American DINER

American DINER

Richard J. S. Gutman and Elliott Kaufman

in collaboration with David Slovic

HARPER & ROW, PUBLISHERS / NEW YORK, HAGERSTOWN, SAN FRANCISCO, LONDON

FIRST EDITION

Book design: Lydia Link

Page layout: Richard J. S. Gutman

Library of Congress Cataloging in Publication Data

Gutman Richard J S
  American diner.
  1. Diners (Restaurants)—United States.
I. Kaufman, Elliott, joint author. II. Slovic, David,
joint author. III. Title.
NA7855.G87 1979   725′.71′0973   79–1665
ISBN 0–06–011698–6

79 80 81 82 83 10 9 8 7 6 5 4 3 2 1

Contents

Acknowledgments

We would like to express our appreciation to those who were of help to us in seeing this project come to fruition:

To Kellie O'Connor Gutman, for her advice and patience during many years of diner hunting and research and writing; to all the diner builders who shared gracefully their experiences and archives, especially Pat and Joe Fodero, Robert and Harold Kullman, Joseph Swingle, and John Cacciatore; to George Mahoney, for providing a very complete record of the Jerry O'Mahony Company; to William D. Wallace, Executive Director of the Worcester Historical Museum, for his generosity in letting us use their collection; to Paul Gray and Norma Holmes, for many long hours of diner discussion and free rein to reproduce items from their extensive collections; to Paula M. Zieselman of the New Rochelle (New York) Public Library, for her research on the Tierneys; to John Baeder, for his enthusiasm and interest in making more people aware of diners.

                    Richard J. S. Gutman

My gratitude to those who were of help in the execution and completion of the photography: Sylvester Cavaletti of Cavy's (Route 30 West, Pennsylvania), Jack Mulholland of the Mayfair Diner (Frankford Avenue, Philadelphia), Frank of Joe's #2 (Route 130 North, New Jersey), and Leo Dalphond of the Old Colony Diner Co. (Dracut, Massachusetts). Warm thanks for cooperation and hospitality go to the diner owners, cooks, waitresses, and customers along Route 1 North and South, Pennsylvania, Route 130 North and South, New Jersey, the Berlin Turnpike, Connecticut, and the Black Horse Pike, New Jersey. Very special thanks to Jeelu Billimoria for her support and faith, peppered with healthy skepticism.

                    Elliott Kaufman

Our gratitude and appreciation to Nach Waxman, without whose unfailing support, encouragement, and expert guidance this book would not have come into being.

American DINER

One nice thing about a diner is that you don't have to tell anyone—no American at least—what it is. To any person who has been raised in our culture, the diner is something totally familiar, as comfortable as the language we speak or the everyday food we eat. Anyone who shares American values and American ways of doing things, anyone who can cope with a gas station or operate a gumball machine, can function here. The assumptions, the atmosphere, the protocols, even the words that are said, are all known.

Physically, the diner is a restaurant of unitary construction, usually longer than it is wide, and it always, *always* has a counter. It has a look we know well—stainless steel and polished mirrors, tile and tough plastic, hard shiny surfaces—cleanable and, thus, we assume, clean. It is a place with a bright polished feel, a place of sunlight pouring in through big glass windows, or, at night, of headlights rushing past, some turning in, flashing for a moment, then going dark as the cars pull up in front.

The diner is a roadside beacon, a message to the traveler that ahead there's welcome relief from tired backs and burning eyes and darkness and the tedious isolation of the highway. It is also a friendly place in town where the "boys" drop in at eleven every morning for coffee and a cruller and to banter a bit with the waitress or counterman. It is an after-school hang out—Cokes and fried onion rings, the juke box, and a good quota of spirited bragging. The diner just seems like a good place to come to. Diners are quick, they're clean, and they're cheap, and best of all they're completely familiar.

They're familiar, of course, because they follow taste, they don't make it. Since the first horse-drawn lunch wagon began peddling sandwiches and coffee to late-night workers back in 1872, the diner—night lunch, night owl, lunch cart, dining car, diner —has always been a faithful reflection of public taste and public need. To see its development is to understand a little more about the country's development and the American idea of what looks and feels good. The pictorial essays in this book tell something about that parallel evolution, tracing the history of the American lunch wagon and stopping along the way to see what was happening in the culture at large, to see the ways in which diners have always thrived by never losing touch with the mainstream of popular taste.

The Birth of the Business

There was once a time when nighthawks, late-night workers and carousers couldn't get anything to eat anywhere in town after 8:00 P.M., when all the restaurants closed for the evening. At least, that was the case in Providence, Rhode Island, before 1872 and the appearance of Walter Scott's first Pioneer Lunch.

Yes, it was Walter Scott who rightfully deserves credit for being the first lunch cart operator. One night in 1872 Scotty trundled down Westminster Street in a light horsedrawn wagon laden with tasty sandwiches, boiled eggs, pies and coffee. This first wagon was merely a converted express wagon. It provided shelter for Scott alone, who sat inside on a wooden box. He had installed a cover, out of which he cut window openings to face both the sidewalk and the street. When customers ordered from the two sides simultaneously Scotty could hand out the victuals and collect the money with both hands.

Scotty served only home-made items. Except for chicken, a nickel could buy any order: a ham sandwich; perhaps a boiled egg with a slice of buttered bread; or a piece of pie—apple, mince, squash, huckleberry or cranberry. For the "dude" trade, there was a plate of sliced chicken at 30 cents. To avoid waste, Scotty invented the "chewed" sandwich, consisting of scraps left over on the cutting board, chopped still finer, and spread with butter or mustard between two slices of bread. For twenty-five years Scotty baked his own bread, and for close to forty his own pies.

At the time of his retirement in 1917, he proudly told the Providence Sunday *Journal,* "For my chicken sandwiches, rooster fowl was always good enough. I bought the best of native birds and cooked them under the best conditions. Nobody ever kicked at a chicken sandwich that I passed out."

As one might expect, the early days were, on occasion, rough and tumble, and Scotty had to devise ways to protect himself against the sorts of rowdies who would eat and run, without paying. Over the years he developed a good eye for judging whether a customer was apt to pay or not. If he distrusted the fellow, Scotty would reach out from the wagon and grab his hat, holding it as security until the bill was paid. He also kept a stout hickory club in case of emergencies. In 1917 Scott reminisced:

> If a man got too gay I had a spring billy that took some of the gayness out of him. Nobody ever wanted more than one taste of the billy. . . .
>
> On another occasion one of the Fox Point roughs tried to beat me out of 10 cents. I took his hat and he took a shot at me with

WALTER
SCOTT.
THE NIGHT
LUNCH CART
PIONEER.

Walter Scott was the founding father of the lunch wagon business. A foodmonger at heart, Scott serviced the stout appetites of Providence night owls around town for nearly sixty years.

his fist. We clinched and rolled to the ground. I fell on top and pounded his head on the pavement until he cried enough. When he got up he asked for his hat.

He didn't get it. My son, who watched the fight, was holding the hat; and he became so nervous that he tore it to pieces without knowing what he was doing. I gave the fellow the pieces and told him that he was lucky to escape so lightly. I heard afterward that he'd served a sentence in State Prison for biting off a man's nose in a fight. I was thankful that he didn't get hold of mine while we were wrestling.

Pushcarts have been used for hundreds of years for hawking food in the streets. John the Orangeman sold his wares from this one at a site near Harvard University. Walter Scott actually started peddling from a basket but quickly switched to this sort of pushcart, making the rounds of newspaper offices, clubrooms, and other spots where people were to be found in the wee hours.

Early Competition

One of the first entrepreneurs to emulate Scotty was a Providence patrolman named Ruel B. Jones. Eight years of night duty in the constabulary convinced Jones that there was a better way to make a living and that there were other lucrative spots in town for a night lunch operator. So sometime in 1883, he turned in his badge and nightstick and by August of that year was operating a healthy business making the rounds to clubrooms and saloons.

Later that year, Jones contracted a local wagon builder named Frank Dracont to construct a wagon for him—the first specifically designed as a lunch cart. It was bright red, with a paneled glass top and an open counter along one side. Business boomed, and by 1887 Jones had a chain of at least seven wagons in Providence. Daily, a caravan of them could be seen winding its way to the Jones house to be stocked up for the night's business.

Before long, competition started to get stiff between lunch cart operators. Mike Stapleton in his wagon at Snow and Westminster Streets was the first to introduce hot dogs, also in the 1880s. Other operators began offering a free slice of onion with an egg sandwich, or catsup, or even mustard, at no extra charge. In fact, it was the high cost of those extras that forced Walter Scott into retirement at the age of seventy-six in 1917:

In 1872, Scotty attached a horse to his mobile food dispensing operation, and the first lunch wagon was born. This horsedrawn rig was a converted freight wagon, providing foul-weather cover for Scott and a handy place to store the previously prepared chow.

But if some of the early patrons were tough customers, few of them wanted the earth for every nickel they spent. If they bought an egg sandwich they didn't demand a slice of onion to go with it. They didn't swamp their beans in catsup or slather mustard on a "dog" until you couldn't see the "dog." In the last few years downtown I lost several dollars a week in free onions, wasted mustard and excess catsup.

I don't know who invented the slice of onion with the fried egg. I know I didn't. With eggs and everything else high, there wasn't much profit in a sandwich at five cents, especially if you added the piece of onion. . . .

I'd probably be in business still if things weren't so high. . . . I guess I've done my share in putting the night lunch on the map, and I'm perfectly willing to step back and let others do the scratching for the dollars that came pretty easy in the old days.

With that, Walter Scott left the lunch cart business.

The First Walk-In Lunch Wagon

Sometime in late 1884 one Samuel Messer Jones, evidently a cousin of Ruel B. Jones, moved from Providence to Worcester, Massachusetts, and made a name for himself there. Although he is often incorrectly credited with conceiving the lunch wagon, Sam Jones did introduce the first one to Worcester, and it also appears that he was the first one to build a wagon that a customer could enter.

Out of work in Providence in 1884, Sam Jones walked home from a lodge meeting one dreary rainy night and spied a lunch wagon with a crowd of people standing around gobbling down some sandwiches and pie. He bought a snack himself, and while he was eating, the night lunch business made a convert. Something else struck him as well, and he wondered why no one had thought of it before—why make people stand out in bad weather to eat? Sam Jones wanted a lunch cart big enough for people to come inside.

With $200 borrowed from a friend, Jones bought an old express wagon which he modified as a lunch cart, but he still didn't have enough money to carry out his idea completely, and his first customers stood outside just like everyone else.

Moving to Worcester shortly afterwards, Jones opened for business on October 20, 1884. Before long, he had accumulated $800, which he invested in a new wagon of his own design. In the fall of 1887 Jones's "first distinctive night lunch wagon" appeared at the New England Fair in Worcester, and, for the first time ever, customers entered a mobile building constructed especially as a lunch cart. The new eatery had a complete kitchen inside, stools for the customers, intricate woodwork and stained glass windows. A newspaper article some years later described them: "Its colored windows were a triumph of the glazier's art, with a bill of fare incorporated in the decorations—sandwiches, pie, cake, coffee and milk."

The idea was an instant success, and Jones expanded his business by adding more wagons at different locations. With the advent of competition, he saw the chance to dispose of his wagons at a good profit and move on. In October of 1889 he sold all his wagons but one to Charles H. Palmer of Worcester.

Both the Park Café and the Brooks' Café worked the streets of Natick, Massachusetts, during the 1890s. The hungry crowds no longer had to stand outside in the rain as they ate their hot dogs. Instead, up to seven people could perch on stools inside in relative comfort; for others, there was standing room.

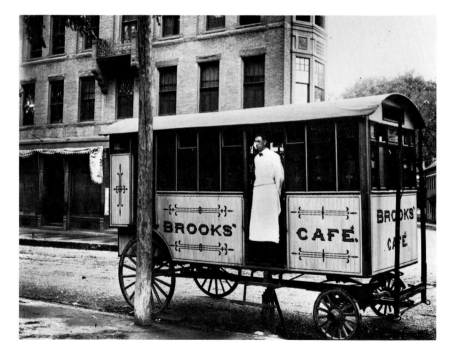

Palmer's Patent

It was in Worcester that the lunch wagon business mushroomed into an industry. On September 1, 1891, Palmer received the first patent given for a lunch wagon design. The patent described what was to become the standard configuration for nearly twenty years: The wagon had an enclosed body with the forward portion extending over a set of small front wheels and the rear made narrower to stand between the tops of the high back wheels.

The rear of the wagon was the "kitchen-apartment," with a counter separating it from the "dining-room space," where customers could sit on stools to eat. Over one of the high rear wheels was a window for passing out food to those customers standing on the curb; the other side had a carriage window where you could drive up to place an order.

Palmer manufactured two models. One was "The Star," a "fancy night café" replete with an elegant ornamental paint job and ringed with stained glass windows etched with—what else?—stars. The other Palmer model was "The Owl." It was described as a "night lunch wagon" and was much simpler in appearance with fewer windows, and those etched with unpretentious designs. Evidently these enclosed carts were extremely popular on cold and stormy nights, but during the summer the crowds preferred to stand out in the open air.

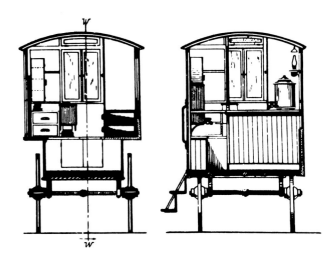

Charles H. Palmer was the first builder to receive a patent on his designs, though they didn't really differ much from what the other manufacturers were producing. His patent drawings show the narrow one-man kitchen over the high rear wheels and the slightly more spacious "dining-room space" in the front half of the wagon.

Charlie Palmer of Worcester broke into the business in 1889 by buying out Sam Jones and his fleet of wagons. Palmer soon started his own manufacturing concern, where he'd build you a solid wagon of standardized dimensions and embellish it according to the size of your pocketbook.

A Gallery of Night Owls

An article in the *New York Times Magazine* of February 7, 1926, prompted by the death the previous year of Sam Jones, the lunch wagon pioneer, described the customers and the milieu of the early wagons.

> Into . . . dull-streeted communities came the lunch wagon, its cheery light shining like a hospitable deed in a chilly world. . . .
>
> Here met all sorts and conditions of men on democratic footing. One would be addressed as "Bo" or "Brother" and only the out-of-place and haughtily supercilious person would resent either term, and such a person had no proper title to admittance and companionship.
>
> Here gathered night workers with an hour to spend in eating and chatting, the night owl who sought sustenance before turning in and he who had no place into which he might turn. Often were found in the company dingy men with a suggestion of the eminence from which they had fallen still irremovably upon them— men who could spout Homer in his own tongue; could discuss philosophies that never made them wise and economies that had failed to enrich them . . .
>
> In the lunch wagon atmosphere one might hear the views of the man on the street on the vital questions—anything and everything from the cross-word puzzle craze to the views of Conan Doyle and Sir Oliver Lodge on life after death and spiritual phenomena. Here gathered the satirist, humorist, raconteur, and over a post-prandial cup of coffee offered leisurely contribution to the discussion.

Wherever crowds gathered you could be sure to find a quick lunch wagon. Old Orchard Beach, Maine, was just such a place, with people promenading, bicycling or just sunning themselves on a nice day.

In the early days, cities such as Providence and Worcester permitted lunch carts to do business on city streets free of charge. Some wagons moved around to the mills, factories and newspaper offices. A slow period was a good time to have your photo snapped in front of your wagon.

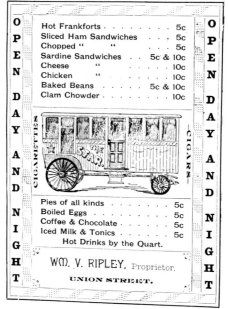

OPEN DAY AND NIGHT

Hot Frankforts	5c
Sliced Ham Sandwiches	5c
Chopped " "	5c
Sardine Sandwiches	5c & 10c
Cheese "	10c
Chicken "	10c
Baked Beans	5c & 10c
Clam Chowder	10c
Pies of all kinds	5c
Boiled Eggs	5c
Coffee & Chocolate	5c
Iced Milk & Tonics	5c
Hot Drinks by the Quart.	

WM. V. RIPLEY, Proprietor.

UNION STREET.

Business boomed for the night lunch trade. Bill Ripley was one of the new operators, who attracted his own clientele by boasting a menu quite extensive for those early days.

Undoubtedly the most eye-catching feature of the lunch wagons was the stained glass window. The windows, such as this one from the Franklin Café in Worcester, were often monogrammed.

Some wagons stayed pretty much in one spot, and customers would drop in after theatre, dances, roller polo games and whist parties. Lunch wagons became fixtures on the streets, providing repasts for revelers and working people alike.

Some smart lunch cart operators opted for locations right where the action was, such as the spot near the Columbia Dance Hall at Salisbury Beach, Massachusetts. Business was terrific on those evenings when there were fifty-cent dances.

Columbia Dance Hall, Salisbury Beach, Mass.

No. 608 Moore & Gibson Co., N. Y. Germany

Here's One "All Wet"

This lunch wagon of ancient date once belonged to William V. Ripley of Oak Bluffs, Massachusetts, on Martha's Vineyard. In 1913 Mr. Ripley sold it to make room for a new one he was purchasing.

The old car was being pulled on shipboard ready for its sail to the mainland and its new owner, when a terrific windstorm came up and blew the ill-fated lunch wagon into the briny deep, where, according to Mr. Ripley, it wallowed about in the surging billows, its big rounded top making it look like a young whale. Wind and tide eventually brought it to where we see it in the picture. We figure the old wagon just naturally liked Oak Bluffs so well that it hated to leave it and hopped overboard and headed for home.

Mr. Ripley tells us the wagon was taken onto the beach, fixed up and eventually reached its new destination, where it sold hot dogs and coffee for many years, until it was replaced with a new car.

The would-be submarine is now down at the water's edge in New Bedford and is used as a boat house where fishermen meet and spin their yarns of the past. But they have to spin some yarn to have anything on this famous old lunch wagon that was once a sea-going "critter" itself.

T. H. Buckley, the Original Lunch Wagon King

Fame and fortune could be made and lost within a few short years in the lunch wagon business, and Thomas H. Buckley, of Worcester, Massachusetts, was without a doubt the preeminent example of a meteoric rise.

Buckley was born on October 21, 1868, in New London, Connecticut. At ten, he moved to Worcester, where he was, successively, a hack driver, an assistant janitor, and a lunch counter boy. In 1888, he built his own first lunch wagon. As in the Sam Jones models, customers could enter Buckley's wagon; its dining area boasted four stools. After being used a number of years in Worcester, this first Buckley wagon was taken to Denver, Colorado, where, under the management of W. A. Bowen, it introduced the quick lunch business to the West.

The reason Buckley built a lunch wagon in the first place was to market his famous oyster stew. As assistant janitor at Horticultural Hall in Worcester, he'd gained quite a reputation dishing up his stew at the dances. However, after building and selling one wagon, he soon decided there was more of a future in constructing lunch carts than in selling stew.

So Tom Buckley committed himself to the manufacture of wagons. By 1892 his firm, the New England Lunch Wagon Company, had built more than seventy-five wagons. After several reorganizations, the outfit emerged in 1898 as the T. H. Buckley Lunch Wagon Manufacturing and Catering Company, with factory and offices at 281 Grafton Street in Worcester. In addition to building lunch carts, they were also dealers in lunch cart supplies, including dishes and urns, Sabatier knives, French plate mirrors and decorated glass, linoleum and wagon jacks.

Although the operators enjoyed terrific success in some New England cities, the carts were slow to take elsewhere. To remedy that situation, Tom Buckley would travel around the countryside choosing towns likely to support lunch wagons. If no one local could be induced into buying one of his eateries, he'd set one up himself, under the direction of a capable hand-picked manager. He wouldn't have to wait long before the wagon could be sold at a handsome profit.

Between 1893 and 1898 Buckley set up wagons in some 275 towns all over the country. In each one he personally appeared before the local council to plead his case for establishing a lunch cart.

The Buckley wagons grew more and more elaborate, the grand designs no longer always fitting the lunch wagon image. In 1897, Buckley opened an incredible restaurant, The White House Café, named after a series of lunch wagons he was promoting at the time.

Not a simple wagon but a massive immobile eatery, it was informally known as "The Delmonico's of Worcester," and was called by The Worcester *Daily Spy,* "the boldest and grandest that has ever been attempted in Worcester." The focus was the fantastic soda fountain made of 18,000 square inches of Mexican onyx. Costing $8000 to build, it sported 36 syrup dispensers. This venture of Buckley's failed miserably, setting him back $25,000. According to one view, The White House Café was "so magnificent in its fittings that it awed everyone. Persons fed themselves by viewing it."

It was said the blow of the restaurant going under broke his health. In any event, on December 1, 1903, Tom Buckley died at the age of thirty-five. Who knows? Maybe it was his gallivanting around the country to those 275 cities and towns promoting lunch wagons that did him in. The T. H. Buckley Company continued just five years after his death.

T. H. Buckley of Worcester, known as the original "Lunch Wagon King," and his colleagues of the New England Lunch Wagon Company built during the 1890s some of the most luxurious lunch carts of all time.

In 1898, Tom Buckley's factory employed 55 craftsmen who worked 14 hours a day just to keep up with the orders. In 10 years they had built some 650 lunch wagons. Except for the painting, a wagon could be completed within 24 to 36 hours, if need be.

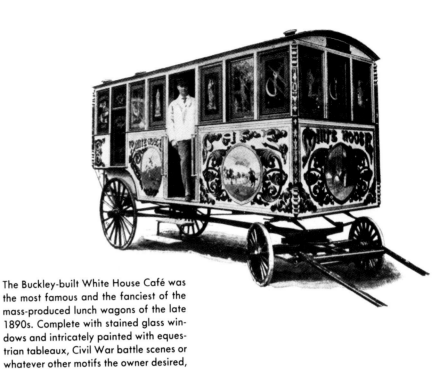

The Buckley-built White House Café was the most famous and the fanciest of the mass-produced lunch wagons of the late 1890s. Complete with stained glass windows and intricately painted with equestrian tableaux, Civil War battle scenes or whatever other motifs the owner desired, these wagons were magnificent sights to behold.

The Celebrated White House Cafés

T. H. Buckley's most famous series of lunch wagons, the White House Cafés, were first introduced on September 4, 1890. They were generally sixteen feet long, six or seven feet wide and ten feet high.

The White House Cafés were quite unlike any other lunch wagons of their day. As one contemporary remarked, "These wagons are perfect little palaces and are admired by all who see them." Each wagon was ringed with windows of red, white, and blue glass. In the plainer models the window glass was etched with scroll designs. More elaborate wagons had "pictured lights," as the stained glass windows were called, some with the four goddesses: Music, Flowers, Day, and Night. Others were etched with portraits of the Presidents: Washington, Lincoln, Grant, Garfield, Harrison, and Cleveland.

The wagons were painted opal white on the outside, and Buckley employed a local artist, C. K. Hardy of Worcester, to embellish them further. Mr. Hardy had many themes: festive hunting scenes, florid landscapes, marine paintings, and works of historical interest. One wagon boasted on the street side a sixteen-foot painting of the Battle of New Orleans. All of the views were surrounded by heavy blue and gold scrolling. The name, "White House Café," was done in heavy block letters.

The Unbelievable Tile Wagon

Back when Tom Buckley began to manufacture lunch wagons, he had the idea of building himself the most elaborate and gorgeous wagon ever made, and on September 28, 1892, after nearly a year's work, the famous "Tile Wagon" was completed. It was used for many years for promotional purposes and sent all over the country to compete in wagon exhibitions, where it invariably won first prize.

Truly a wonder, the Tile Wagon was constructed on the inside entirely of tiling. As Buckley himself described it, "The floor is laid in mosaic tile of fine design, and the entire ceiling and walls are covered with a bright, glistening opal tiling, inserted in which are artistic designs of numerous flashing brilliants."

The interior was lit by lamps with bases incorporating ivory and gold statuettes of historical figures, mounted on ebony pedestals. The patrons sat on nickeled stools with glass tops as they ate their food and appreciated what Buckley called the "fine workmanship in the historical art. . . . Washington with his cloak thrown carelessly about him, stands as though viewing his army; Lincoln with his pen in hand has just signed the Emancipation Proclamation; . . . and Columbus, gazing into the distance, points down at a revolving globe by his side." Other statuettes included an American newsboy and a violinist.

"The most elaborate cash register ever built" was prominently located behind the counter, which had a top of heavy polished brass. Spittoons made of brass helped complete the interior appointments.

The exterior was covered with heavy beveled German and French plate glass mirrors inlaid with lacework tracery. A pair of hammered silver carriage lamps adorned the front of the wagon.

Buckley claimed the Tile Wagon, built at a cost of $5,440, was worth to him a quarter of a million dollars in advertising. It certainly did help the public open its eyes and take a second look at lunch wagons, although it was far too costly and elaborately decorated to serve practically as an eating establishment. According to Jim Harrington, who ran a Buckley cart in Waterbury, Connecticut, in the 1890s, "People thought the man was crazy to put so much money into a cart."

Buckley Wagons Fight Demon Rum

The Buckley lunch wagons received publicity in one unusual way. Early on, several were sold to the Church Temperance Society, under whose proprietorship they offered stiff competition to the free lunch that was offered in most bars during the 1890s. At that time, a man could go into a saloon, buy a couple of beers for a dime, and partake of a free lunch that included pig's feet, ham, beans, bread and other tidbits. The Church Temperance Society, in Tom Buckley's lunch carts, proceeded to serve meat, vegetables and coffee for that same thin dime. The price was far too low to make this much of a business proposition, but it was not too cheap for a moral issue. In fact, a customer who had only a few pennies could get two pancakes and a cup of coffee for three cents, or, for the same sum, buy a serving of rice pudding. Soup and bread without butter was a mere six cents. The Church Temperance Society was composed of prominent and influential clergy and laymen of the Protestant Episcopal Church. Proceeds from the wagons were used to build free ice water fountains in the tenement districts of New York City.

It was the Church Temperance Society that introduced the first lunch wagon in 1893 to the business area of New York City. "The Owl" was the name of the wagon, and it was located at Herald Square, right in front of the *Herald* Building. It just so happened that the facade of the *Herald* Building was adorned with decorative owls. "The Owl" wagon had no connection with the *Herald,* but the scathingly wry comments of publications like *Life* magazine prompted the *Herald* to ask the Temperance Society to move its wagon.

The Temperance wagons were made possible by endowments from a number of prominent New Yorkers, among them Cornelius Vanderbilt, who was quoted in the *New York Times Magazine* of December 24, 1922, as saying, "I like these restaurants on wheels. When you want one come to me." Mr. Vanderbilt provided a wagon, and its name ("Good Cheer"), which was installed on the east side of Union Square.

By 1898 there were eight Temperance wagons in the city, some of which were called The Way-Side Inn. In a single year they supplied 230,804 ten-cent meals. Buckley claimed the sixteen-by-seven-foot interior was capable of serving twenty-five people at one time. Unlike the White House Cafés, the Temperance wagons were finished in natural wood with heavy lettering in blue and gold. The stained glass windows had the Church Temperance Society's monogram on each pane.

The Church Temperance Society Window and other examples of stained glass artistry were featured in the Buckley catalog.

Tom Buckley was proud to pose in 1898 beside one of his Temperance lunch wagons.

Off-Street Dining

Lunch wagons became so popular in New England shortly after the turn of the century that in Providence, for example, nearly fifty of the "floating" restaurants were roaming the streets by 1912. It wasn't long, however, before all of those "two frankforts and a cup o' coffee for a nickel" wagons started to become eyesores, their gaily painted exteriors fading and peeling in a few years to a lackluster weatherworn finish. Also, with scores of customers hopping in and out on a nightly basis, the light-weight lunch wagons soon literally opened at the seams.

Citizen complaints began in earnest when some wagons stayed on into the late morning to do more business, a clear violation of their operating permits, because the early lunch carts were only allowed to remain on the streets from dusk till dawn. So the cities cracked down and declared that the wagons had to be off the streets by 10 A.M. A number of operators quickly discovered a good way around the rules.

The simplest answer was to pick a good site, off the road, where the lunch carts could set up permanently.

For most owners life was considerably simpler once the wagons became permanently situated and the need to trundle them around town was eliminated. Supporting the romantic image of the horse-drawn lunch cart was really a lot of trouble, and soon most everybody was happy to abandon it.

Thus occurred the greatest change in the history of the business —the transformation of the wandering horsedrawn wagon into the stationary (yet still portable) diner.

Once the wagons were off the streets, they were not restricted to specific hours, and, in order to capitalize on the hungry masses, many stayed open around the clock. Not only did the business profit, but the public appreciated being able to grab a bite, any hour, day or night.

The name "street cafés" for lunch wagons became an anachronism during the first decade of the century, when the first lunch carts began to set up on their own parcels of land. Wagons like this one in Mansfield, Massachusetts, no longer appeared nightly at the curb, but moved a few paces off the streets to permanent locations.

When the lunch wagons left the streets, some owners felt they no longer needed mobility. In 1911, F. E. Eberling of Clifton, New Jersey, plopped his Quick Lunch (above), sans wheels, on a low foundation in an empty lot. The wagon below, in Plainfield, New Jersey, is from the same period, but evidently kept its wheels, which were boxed in behind wooden paneling.

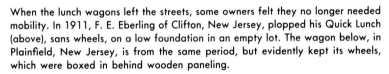

The new permanent locations led rapidly to the establishment of many lunch wagons as 24-hour businesses. Owners made a big to-do about throwing away their keys, and new signs on the wagons read, "We Never Close," "Always Open," "Open Day and Night." The permanent locations also permitted a wide expansion of the menu. With water, gas, electrical and sewage connections, the preparation of a greater range of cooked foods was made much easier, and ham and eggs, steaks, chops and roasts began to appear with some frequency on the bill of fare.

13

ANOTHER SUCCESS STORY

By 1913 the dining car was entering a new era, and Jerry O'Mahony of Bayonne, New Jersey, realized it. At age 33 Jerry was still working in his father's bar and grill. Owners of local lunch cars often stopped by for a beer, and, as Jerry's son George relates, of all the people patronizing the establishment, the least to worry about were the dining car operators: When the time came to pick up the tab, they invariably pulled giant wads of bills from their pockets. This image of the highly successful dining car operator had a strong influence upon him, and Jerry decided to have a go at the lunch wagon business himself. He bought a car, was immediately successful, and expanded until he figured the only way was to build them himself.

In 1913 Jerry set up shop in a small garage in Bayonne, vowing to construct the most beautiful and the most rugged lunch cars available. At that time most dining cars were pretty flimsy, so when a customer from northern New England came to the O'Mahony plant, he wanted solid proof that that their product could withstand a harsh climate with heavy snow. Jerry didn't hesitate. He called his workers and ordered them onto the roof of a finished diner. The skeptic, having seen all he needed, left with a new O'Mahony lunch car.

The O'Mahony company built only low-wheeled permanently installed cars, and eventually became the largest manufacturer of the time. Soon Jerry was unabashedly claiming, "In our line, we lead the world."

An important design change occurred when the wagons began to be set up on permanent sites. Instead of having high wheels in the back, they were built with two sets of low wheels. Originally, when the wagons were making daily trips through narrow, muddy, rutted streets, high wheels were a necessity, even though they used up valuable kitchen space. Now wheels were needed only to get from factory to site, and to change locations when necessary. The American Eagle Café, built in 1910 by a new outfit, the Worcester Lunch Car Company, shows the low-wheeled look and also introduces a new roof design featuring a raised clerestory with operable windows. At the same time, the need for bigger diners that could accommodate the wider menu and more customers led to a repositioning of the counter and a lengthening of the lunch wagon. The new scheme placed the kitchen along the length of the car with a long serving and eating counter running down the middle. As the lunch cars grew longer, the size of the kitchen was increased in direct proportion to the seating, as shown in this interior view.

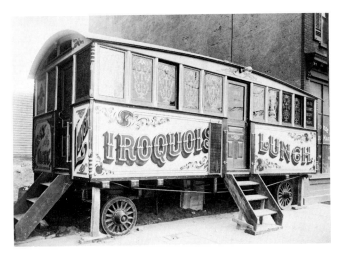

When diners were placed on location, the wheels, more often than not, remained. Occasionally they were buried in the ground, serving as the foundation. Often they were merely hidden by wood or brick. As long as they remained, the wheels gave protection against building codes, because technically the diner remained a wagon and not a building. This sequence of O'Mahony-built diners from around 1915 shows the steps taken toward making the wagons permanent. All versions kept their wheels; some just looked more stationary than others. If business dropped off, the wagon could easily move to another site. The different foundations were merely efforts to make the lunch cars look more formidable.

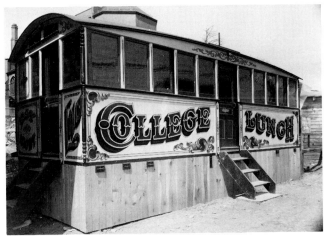

The long, narrow shape of the lunch cars allowed them to occupy slivers of land that were virtually unusable for any conventional building. The rents were therefore extremely low. The Walkor Lunch was located in a high-traffic spot opposite New York's Pennsylvania Station, on a long, narrow lot that was ideal for a lunch car. The Lenox Lunch was slapped down in front of a synagogue, right on the sidewalk. Like the newsstand next to it, this early diner commanded but a fragment of space. At least one enterprising proprietor, named Harvey, even gave up his front yard to squeeze a diner in front of his house.

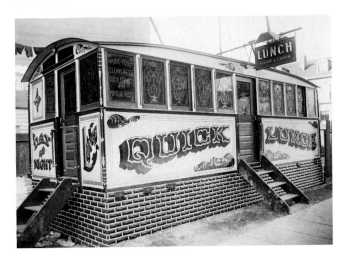

The Age of the Trolley-Lunch

Just around the turn of the century, the lunch wagon rage suffered its first major setback. In city after city the traditional horsedrawn trolleys were being replaced by electric streetcars, and not only the transit companies' car barns, but empty lots all over town, began filling with these battered old wrecks. Soon the companies began to sell them off for a pittance to anyone who would haul them away. Once the pride of their cities, the discarded horse trolleys were converted by their new owners into chicken coops, newspaper stands, housing, and—what else?—immobile lunch wagons. With a little elbow grease and some paint and about fifty dollars' worth of equipment—a counter and stools, a coffee urn, a grill and some dishes—a fellow had himself a lunch car. Nothing, though, could mask the shoddy state of these scarred old trolleys.

Their effect was absolutely devastating. For the first time a stigma, growing out of the influx of the disreputable-looking trolley-lunches, began to be attached to the lunch wagon. Until the advent of the surplus trolleys, lunch carts had been considered perfectly respectable places to go to for a quick meal and were patronized by all types of people.

It is true, of course, that, because of their hours, lunch carts were, right from the beginning, favorite haunts of those who were out drinking the night away. A drawing of an inebriated soul steadying himself against a brick wall accompanied an article entitled "The Night Lunch Business" in the Springfield *Graphic* of April 29, 1893. It began with some verse:

> Often on a midnight dreary
> Rounders muddle with the query
> Where they'll go to get a soberfying, satisfying bite:
> White House, Palace, Ruth, Oasis, Nox, or wheeless
>   midnight places,
> And then unto the nearest one they make erratic flight.

In actual fact the occasional drunk never really kept the good customers away from the lunch wagons. The converted trolleys, though, with their dark corners, drafts, and leaky roofs, surely did. Unattractive and uninviting to the general public, they began to cater to an even less reputable type of night trade. The police helped to reinforce the bad image of the trolley-lunches, as they were always sure to include

them on their rounds while looking for shady characters and desperate underworld types who just might have committed crimes. By the late 1890s, even the better carts were getting a bad reputation, and the lunch wagon business was caught in a uphill battle, one that has continued to plague diners to this day.

The Lackawanna Trail Lunch Car in Stroudsburg, Pennsylvania, a converted horse-drawn trolley, was about as dingy a place as you could get. Small, cramped and drafty, the trolley shown in this tattered old snapshot is a prime example of how the bad image in diners surfaced around 1900. Many people came to believe diners and old trolleys were one and the same.

On Route 1 near Berwyn, Maryland, the Maxwell Diner, a trolley-lunch photographed in 1940, offered outdoor service by opening the car's front windows.

Mullen's Dining Cars in Buellton, California, was built in 1947 from two retired L.A. streetcars. This was Ray Mullen's ingenious and inexpensive solution to the postwar construction material shortage.

NEW LIVES FOR OLD STREETCARS

Off and on for the next forty years, relics from the street railway systems of many cities were pressed into service as trolley-lunches, often calling themselves diners. Although some of these trolleys were restored and kept up rather nicely, most were not, and the stigma persisted. The brief era of the trolley-lunch generated the still widespread myth that all diners—at least older ones—are converted trolley cars.

Ray's Lunch near Natick, Massachusetts, was an ex-trolley transplanted into a startlingly idyllic setting.

Those Fabulous Diner-a-Day Tierneys

The liveliest dinner in dining car history—July 10, 1925—wasn't in a diner. That night the Tierney sons Ned and Dick, second-generation diner builders, celebrated the opening of their new factory in New Rochelle, New York, with a dinner for close to 1000 people given in their plant. Many speeches were made praising the boys and their father and mother. The toastmaster, Edward Cordial, mentioned in his opening remarks that if he tried to talk about the Tierneys, he could go on for a year, and then only touch the surface.

It was an evening not to be missed. George Bayright, speaking on behalf of the Tierney employees, said they considered the reception to be one of the greatest events of their lives. Time and again the glorious accomplishments of P. J. Tierney and his sons were extolled. To illustrate how far they had come in the business, George Bayright reminisced:

We all remember when the lunch wagon business was not considered a business, when a horse was attached to the wagon and it was stealthily drawn to some advantageous spot to dole out meager rations to the wayfarer, to again be carted away to an obscure corner at the break of day. Tonight's reception is the most convincing evidence of the growth of this business.

The evening was a testimonial to the phenomenal success of the P. J. Tierney Sons Company, which had become the largest manufacturer of diners in the world. Their great new plant was turning out a diner a day, and all those cars sold like hotcakes, because the name Tierney had become synonymous with diner.

The Tavern Grill, a 1925 Tierney Diner, was typical of what the P. J. Tierney Sons were turning out one of every day. This model had as a special feature a canvas sunscreen which, along with the awnings, helped to keep the inside temperature down during the hot summer months.

This Quick Lunch was a Tierney car brought in especially for the Hotel Exposition in Atlantic City, New Jersey, in 1924. It sat right on the Boardwalk, providing quick meals for the tourists and great publicity for the Tierneys. This unusual rear view shows Dick Tierney himself in the right foreground.

The Man Who Brought the Toilet Inside

Patrick Joseph "Pop" Tierney brought new stability to the lunch wagon business at a crucial time. Back in the early 1900s when the trolley-lunches were giving all diners a bad name, P. J. Tierney of New Rochelle, New York, embarked on the manufacture of lunch wagons. He built so many good ones that he helped overshadow the bad image and restored to the diner its lost respectability.

It wasn't at all long before Tierney was selling more lunch cars than anyone else around. He loved lunch wagons and would do practically anything to get someone started running his own. If he liked you, you'd pay one-fourth down and the rest on time. If he liked you a lot and you had an old lunch wagon (if you had an old lunch wagon he'd almost surely like you a lot), he'd take the wagon as down payment. And if he loved you, he'd give you a new wagon, and all you had to do was promise to pay for it.

P. J. Tierney made it his business to get out among the people and sell his diners personally. It was for this purpose that he traveled to Greenwich, Connecticut, on January 10, 1917. One Mrs. Benham of Yonkers accompanied him, and they inspected there a lunch wagon similar to one she intended to buy. After supper at the diner, they returned to Yonkers. Upon entering Mrs. Benham's home, Mr. Tierney complained of gas pains in his stomach. He took a dose of Bromo Seltzer and was persuaded to lie down while a doctor was summoned. But when the physician arrived, Mr. Tierney was dead. He had died within ten minutes of lying down, and acute indigestion was given as the cause.

When Pop Tierney died a millionaire, his sons Ned and Dick, who had grown up with the business, took over. They tried in their advertising to build their father into a legend:

> It was Patrick J. Tierney, the founder of the *Dining Car Business of America,* who was the first to take the *Dining Car* off the street and to give it a permanent location. . . . It was Patrick J. Tierney who first conceived the idea of equipping the *Car* with tile. . . . It was he who first installed exhaust fans, skylights and ventilators and who replaced the old kerosene lamps by electric lights.

And it was also Patrick J. Tierney who brought the toilet inside. Although his sons, it appears, were not especially interested in this claim, there is little doubt that many patrons over the years were highly appreciative.

The first Tierney plant, situated unimposingly behind Pop's home, turned out just three lunch carts its first year. This little workshop was a far cry from the highly touted factory built by his sons in 1925. That shop employed 250 men working on 40 diners at a time.

The P. J. Tierney Sons Company left a complete photographic record of their construction process in 1924. In the first stage, workmen are shown laying the frame for a diner built right on its wheels.

After the wall panels and roof were installed, the electricians wired the car. Work then progressed with the building of the counter and shelves and sheathing the side walls and ceiling. Once the counter was finished, the marble top was put in place and the tile was laid.

With everything in place except for the tops of the stools, a final coat of varnish finished the interior.

Meanwhile, on the outside the painting crew was hard at work covering the diner in white enamel and embellishing it with gold lettering.

Lookalike Lunch Cars

P. J. Tierney Sons thought they had the market pretty well cornered in the early twenties, but in fact two other outfits were snapping at their heels. By the early teens the Worcester Lunch Car Company of Worcester, Massachusetts, was doing well enough that Pop Tierney sent some people up to Worcester posing as potential buyers. They toured the plant and returned to New Rochelle with information on the competition's latest improvements. And closer to home was the Jerry O'Mahony Company of Bayonne, New Jersey. With plenty of Tierney Diners in neighboring towns, it was easy for Jerry and his boys to keep tabs on Tierney innovations, and vice versa. The result of all this spying and copying was a lot of different diners that all looked pretty much the same.

Walking through the sliding door into the middle of any of these diners, the customer was struck instantly by the long marble counter. In the more elaborate models he saw a dazzling, almost dizzy combination of ceramic tile designs on the walls and floor. As natural light streamed through the skylights and etched and frosted windows, it was reflected off the shiny metal coffee urns onto the ceiling of highly varnished wood or brightly painted metal. The stools were wholly constructed of white porcelain enamel, sometimes topped with wooden or leather seats.

Because it was pretty difficult to tell these diners apart, each outfit developed hard-sell slogans to promote their cars. Worcester declared, "In New Jersey they've got class, but we build them to last." Ned and Dick stated simply, "Tierney Diners Make Money." Jerry O' unabashedly claimed, "In our line, we lead the world." As a matter of fact, it really didn't matter whose diner you bought. In the 1920s, with nearly any new diner you would slice yourself a nice piece of the pie.

These two Worcester Lunch Cars, the Franklin in Attleboro, Massachusetts (above), and the Kitchenette in Cambridge, Massachusetts (below), are typical of the mid-twenties. Both boasted fancy paint jobs with elaborate scrollwork and pin-striping and a double row of counters for extra seating.

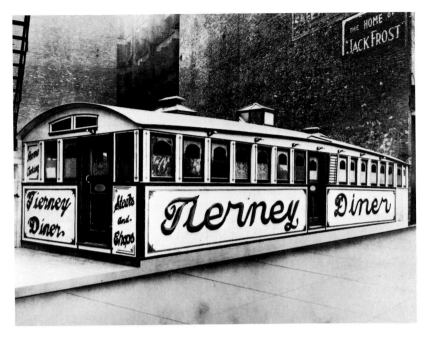

Terhune's Palace Café in East Rutherford, New Jersey (above and below), was a Jerry O'Mahony offering from the 1920s. It is distinguished mainly by the fact that it had two doors on the front and a counter of white marble.

This Tierney Diner (above and below) was located at 14th and Hudson Streets in New York City. Its deluxe floor was almost a Persian carpet in tile. As with most 1920s diners Tierney cars came complete with dishes, silverware, pots and pans.

Diners on the Move

Up until the mid-twenties nearly all diners were put on flatcars and shipped by rail to their destinations. The average car at that time was thirty feet long and no more than ten and a half feet wide; anything over that ten and a half feet couldn't be accommodated by the railroad. Diner lore has it that it was a mistake in dimensioning by a manufacturer who built a car wider than the railroad could move that brought dining car trucking into its own.

Truckers were already being used to some extent in the early twenties for moving cars from the railroad tracks to the site, but no one other than the P. J. Tierney Sons Company ever trucked the car all the way from factory to site. Most plants were built right next to the railroad tracks, but the Tierney plant was an exception. Located two or three miles from the nearest railroad, they had their own in-house trucking operation. Unfortunately their trucks always seemed to be breaking down, and invariably help was needed to get them back on the road. George and Frank Parker, identical twins from New Rochelle, New York, usually answered the call. They started in the garbage business, but were good mechanics and helped the Tierneys out of so many scrapes that in 1924 they gave up hauling garbage and started moving diners full time.

Ten miles per hour was the limit during the move by road. Otherwise vibrations were set up that could seriously hurt the diner. Also, the tires and wheels would heat up too much at greater speeds. The Parker brothers told a story of moving a diner the short distance from New Rochelle to Bridgeport, Connecticut, a run that should have taken five hours or so. However, because of overloading they ended up burning out the hubs on twenty-seven wheels, and the move dragged on for four days.

More than once the unexpected would occur to make life miserable for the dining car truckers. Frank Parker once backed a diner four miles because someone told him a bridge outside Little Falls, New York, had a safe clearance of sixteen feet; all it turned out to have was fourteen feet six inches. In the later years, when pneumatic tires came into use, a little air could always be let out in such a situation, or the wheels could be removed and the car could creep forward on six-inch rollers. If that proved of no avail, there always was the back-up method, but that wasn't much fun with twenty tons blocking your view and being ornery every foot of the way.

By the late twenties dining car trucking had become an industry within an industry, populated by two-fisted, cantankerous roustabouts like this crew who moved Worcester Lunch Cars.

DINERS BY
LAND AND SEA

Up through the twenties all diners were built right on iron wheels. All the movers had to do was hook them up to their rigs and they were ready to hit the road. When shipping was to be carried out by rail, the wheels were removed for that part of the journey, and the diner would be bolted to the flatcar. However, this method still shook up the diner and did more damage than trucking. If the easiest route was over water, the diner would be lifted by crane onto a barge. Crowds usually gathered to witness the event. During the twenties a few diners bound for California went this way via the Panama Canal.

THE GILDED AGE

1872 - 1918

The years following the Civil War were prosperous ones. Huge fortunes were amassed, and with their lifestyle the ostentatious rich set a highly visible example for the rest of the country. The public was enthralled with the homes and the haunts of the wealthy—with places the likes of the Palmer House in Chicago, where the floor of the barber shop was inlaid with silver dollars. Luxury and up-to-date elegance were epitomized by the new Pullman Palace Cars with their rich inlaid woods, scroll work, velvet, tassels, and tinted windows.

When, as was inevitable, this mentality was translated into architecture and furnishings, the gingerbread age was born. Everywhere there was an overload of ornamental detail, from the fancy jigsaw fretwork of house exteriors to the dripping interiors, with room after room overcrowded by plush and fringe, hung with heavy draperies, and festooned with knick-knacks.

It was a fanciful and sentimental era, when city parks were carefully landscaped and manicured into romantic disorder, and rugs were woven to reproduce as exactly as possible idyllic landscape paintings.

The last part of the nineteenth century saw a boom in mass production, especially of furniture, with machines being employed to recreate the art of the craftsman. Imitative designs were common, as objects made of metal were stamped and finished to simulate wood, and others made of plastics could easily be mistaken for tortoise shell, marble, ivory or mother-of-pearl.

The machine-made objects were meant to look handcrafted. In fact, the new methods of machine production allowed designers an easier time in applying ornament, with the paradoxical result that ordinary pieces of furniture were also works of art. Of course, alternative, simple styles of furniture did surface—and some became quite popular. One, whose heyday was around the turn of the century, was the Mission style, built of sturdy, spare, functional oak. Mission remained in favor until the First World War, but it was the "art" furniture, intricately, elaborately and overly detailed, that the majority of Americans continued to live with.

This 1870s photograph (above) taken inside the Commonwealth Avenue home of a proper Bostonian shows furnishings and assemblages typical of the period: lots of bric-a-brac, draped rugs, sculpture and ornately turned furniture. The highly ornamental art organ (below) would not be out of place in such a Victorian home.

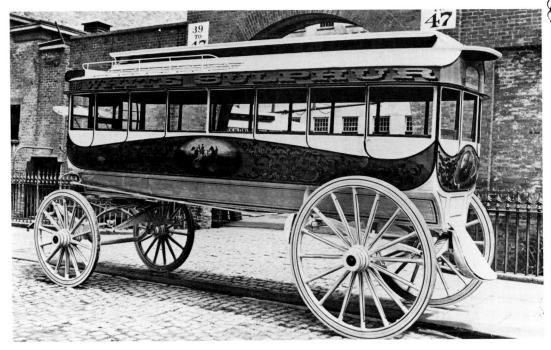

Edward Bok, turn-of-the-century editor of the *Ladies' Home Journal* and long-time crusader against Victorian excesses, attributed the low taste of Americans directly to Pullman cars and their ostentatiousness.

This intricately painted vehicle (above) is believed to have been constructed in the 1870s for the celebrated White Sulphur Springs Hotel in West Virginia by the John Stevenson Company, a leading builder of horsedrawn trolleys and omnibuses. The T. H. Buckley lunch wagon (below), built in the 1890s, owed some of its carnival inspiration to the railroad and trolley, as well as to circus cars and Mississippi river boats with their white paneling and florid carving. The brightly colored stained glass in the diner reflects the general popularity of colored glass in homes and commercial buildings, not to mention its use in railroad and streetcars.

An elaborate lamp such as this one by C. H. Covell of New York City would fit into any Victorian interior of the 1880s. Not only did it provide illumination—it was intended to be a piece of art. The gas lamps of Tom Buckley's famous Tile Wagon lunch cart surely were inspired by models such as this.

What! No Women?

By the mid-twenties there was still a large segment of the American population that had never even seen the inside of a diner. The ruffian image that had been with the lunch carts practically from the beginning seemed to say "men only," and the women did pretty much keep their distance. But business was business and all those women who weren't coming to diners meant good dollars that weren't making it to the till. So here and there signs began to be seen announcing "Ladies Invited," and while these didn't exactly pack the cars, they were an indication of progress. Soon a number of operators started going out more actively after women, sending handbills to all the nearby offices. Then, gradually, small touches began to appear, designed to attract the ladies. Flowerboxes and shrubs added an appealing touch on the exterior. Frosted glass windows insured privacy from ogling passersby. And most important, a wider variety of foods began to appear on the menu to give the new customers a bit more of a choice.

When the dining car owners discovered a sure-fire method to draw in women, they frequently shared their good-luck stories. An operator from Pennsylvania reported how one time an O'Mahony service man dropped in with his family to see how things were going. The O'Mahony man sat his family (wife, mother, and three little girls) right by the front door, which he propped open. When the operator asked, "What's the big idea? Want to let in the flies?," the fellow replied that it was a trick to attract women. And sure enough, when two women passed by a few minutes later, they stopped to look. One said to the other, "Why, women do eat in there, Sarah. Look, there's some real nice ladies and three little girls, too. Let's go in." That was the start of that particular operator's "women business." Soon he didn't even have to seat his women customers by the door.

The increased patronage by women prompted one major design innovation. One of the reasons women had seldom gone into dining cars was that they just didn't feel comfortable perched up on stools. To remedy this, manufacturers started to offer diners with tables or booths.

While some operators were after the female clientele, others definitely were not. The question of women and dining cars was so hotly debated that it was made the subject of a monthly feature in the early issues of Jerry O'Mahony's magazine, *Dining Car News.* A letter in the issue of February, 1927 clearly shows just how strongly some dinermen felt about the subject:

The simple fact was that women seldom patronized dining cars. This view (above) of a hearty discussion going on between men, not only dressed in overalls but smoking, helped to reinforce the image of the diner as a workingmen's place. Working women (inset) tended to take their noon meals at such establishments as Horn and Hardart or other cafeterias, where they were more comfortable.

TO THE EDITOR: What, No Woman department:

I think you're all wet on the "What, No Woman" question. Their money is as good as any man's, as you say, and there may be locations where women will bring in big jack, but not for me.

I got a location, a good one too, down by the piers, and while a lady's safe enough in my car, she'll hear some cuss words that'll turn her ears pink. What do you think about that, Mr. Editor?

J. B., New York.

The editor admitted that maybe J. B.'s was one case where women were "out."

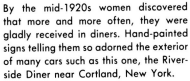

By the mid-1920s women discovered that more and more often, they were gladly received in diners. Hand-painted signs telling them so adorned the exterior of many cars such as this one, the Riverside Diner near Cortland, New York.

Because women supposedly didn't feel at ease perched on the ordinary diner stools with their thin, pancake tops, some owners installed fancy stools with backs. These might be made of cane, upholstered leather or even mahogany.

In 1926, the diner makers began to bring out their new models, which provided both stool and table service, "a feature particularly attractive to feminine patronage," as manufacturer Jerry O'-Mahony put it in one of his brochures.

In 1927, owner Eugene Flamm offered photographic proof that even with counter service only, it was still possible to crowd your car with women. The Flamm Dining Car was located in Brooklyn right around the corner from a vaudeville house, and the girls were regulars.

A Home Away from Home

A unique feeling of camaraderie developed in many diners, something not seen in any other sector of the restaurant business. One reason for this was the diner's normal twenty-four-hour operation. Any time, day or night, you could count on getting a bite to eat in a warm, casual atmosphere down at your local lunch wagon.

Right from the start, diners became centers of social life. In the small town of Waverly, New York, there was one particular diner called the Men's Lunch. Two brothers, Bill and Ed O'Brien, had bought the car in 1926 and almost instantly initiated a "Coffee Club," which became a daily informal meeting place where local businessmen could get together to talk over politics and local events.

The most popular topic of discussion at the Coffee Club was, in fact, the weather, so Ed O'Brien started to bone up on the subject. One thing led to another, and soon Ed had gone and bought himself $1500 worth of equipment: a barometer, wind gauges, thermometers, and so on. It got to the point where Ed finally found himself appointed an official weather observer by the United States Weather Bureau. And each day dozens of friends and customers would phone the diner to get the forecast before embarking on a trip or hanging out the wash.

Not only did the Coffee Club fill the Men's Lunch in the morning, crowds of young people packed the car after school. Every local football game was carefully analyzed, usually with the aid of chalk diagrams on the floor.

Bill and Ed also had one other nice touch at their diner. They always gave a hungry man a sandwich and a cup of coffee. In return the fellow would sweep the sidewalk out front.

The Men's Lunch is only one example of the diner social style. Most diners, in fact, have a spirit quite different from that of the ordinary lunch room, a "clubby" atmosphere of friendly and informal good fellowship.

Some workingmen would eat lunch at the same spot, day in, day out, year after year—and for these a diner offered just the right atmosphere. This crowd is made up of some of the regulars at one of Harry Zelin's Market Diners in New York City around 1940.

Always, but especially on a snowy wintry night in December 1948, a local lunch car like Sully's in Taunton, Massachusetts, provided a cheery haven for those out and about.

Smiles Over The Counter

The regulars always seemed to love posing in front of their diners. This was true even in the days of the old lunch wagons (left), as shown by the Boys' Glee Club from the Oak Bluffs Baptist Church hamming it up on Martha's Vineyard, Massachusetts. John and Bill's Diner (above) sponsored the Junior Drum Corps of Derry, New Hampshire, so naturally the whole gang turned out for the group portrait on the steps of the diner. An impromptu photo-taking session (right) might well pull everyone out onto the sidewalk, as can be seen in this picture of Sam's in Hammonton, New Jersey.

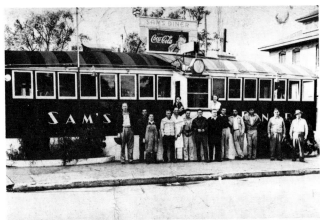

The World's Largest Diner

The 1920s was the first boom period for dining cars. With the Tierney Sons Company turning out a diner a day and the O'Mahony outfit achieving nearly as impressive an output, new diners were popping up not only in the cities and towns but along the highways as well. This was the beginning of the age of the roadside diner, which sprang up to feed the flood of autoists traveling the new motorways.

Within the city, chauffeurs, laborers, mechanics and clerks were heading in ever greater numbers for diners. They had half an hour off for lunch and knew that in a dining car they could eat and be out in ten minutes. Businessmen also patronized the lunch cars, not so much for their speed as for their good chow. And, with the ever-growing number of women customers, many cars were often packed to overflowing.

As a result, diners began to grow in size, and the competition for bigger diners became very heated. Soon the race was on, as dinermen and manufacturers sought to attract the attention of the eating public by offering "The World's Largest Diner." It was, of course, a never-ending process, because the next one along could always be 5 feet longer. The problem was generally not one of making a larger car but of transporting the new super-long diner to its site.

The quest for "The World's Largest Diner" has continued to this day. However, in 1941 a technique called split construction was developed by Paramount Diners, permitting a diner to be built in two parts, which were shipped separately and then clipped together on site. This breakthrough meant that diners could be made of any number of units, so the constraints on size that had been imposed by shipping requirements disappeared. Today's world's largest diner, the Country Club in Philadelphia, was built by Fodero. Consisting of twenty sections and covering a phenomenal 10,000 square feet, it is not likely to be outdone in the near future.

The Bayway had to be a big one. Brought in by the Standard Oil Company in 1926 to be located outside their refinery in Bayway, New Jersey, this diner helped to feed 3000 employees a day on their 'round-the-clock shifts.

Although 5000 people may have flocked to the opening of this large new diner, it is inconceivable that they could all have received even as much as a cup of coffee. It is true that in the twenties diners were very popular, but a little promotional hyperbole seems at work here.

It was claimed that Elmer C. Wightman of Attleboro, Massachusetts, had the "most prosperous dining car location in the world." And, of course, it goes without saying that he also had the world's largest diner.

LOCATED AT THE JUNCTION OF ROUTES 21 AND 20,

BOSTON POST ROAD, SPRINGFIELD, MASS.

Sam's Diner made a more limited claim to fame, but the fact was that around 1930 diners still rarely existed outside of New England. Not only that, but super-long ones didn't make it too far from the factories where they were built in Massachusetts, New York and New Jersey.

With the birth of split construction, diners began to be built in any number of parts and put together on location. Pretty soon the notion of the world's largest diner became meaningless. The size of the diner was limited only by the ambition of the owner and the area of his lot. This 1946 photograph shows the two halves of the Tastee Diner in Silver Spring, Maryland, being hooked together.

The world's largest diners invariably came to include gimmicks other than sheer size alone. One short-lived corny touch of the thirties was the inclusion of a fireplace in a few cars. It probably did little to make the diner seem more romantic.

The separate dining room became a standard feature of most of the world's largest diners. After all, you could only use so much counter space, so in the case of some popular cars such as the Rainbow Grill, a dining room addition was brought in to cope with the crowds.

The Les Crater Diner was a 1930s attempt to place two cars side by side and make them look like one big wide diner. Only the dip in the roofline where the cars meet gives a clue to the construction.

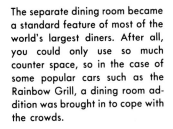

Thinking Small

While the general trend in diners over the years has been toward bigger and bigger cars, not everybody has preferred the giant new deluxe models. Both customers and owners who had grown up during the era of the lunch wagon felt more at home in the cozy confines of a nice small diner. As a result, a new demand for small units developed around 1936 or 1937. Depression conditions undoubtedly also contributed to a return to the early days of the dining car—a one-man operation with a limited menu made economic good sense in tough times.

These new "dinettes" were designed especially for the short order trade, with its call for lighter dishes and lunch and dinner specialties. Now, instead of patronizing the older worn-out wagons, customers seeking an intimate diner could find just what they wanted—and brand, spanking new at that! People flocked to these mini units, some of which continued to look like diners, if perhaps a little more flashy to make up for the difference in size.

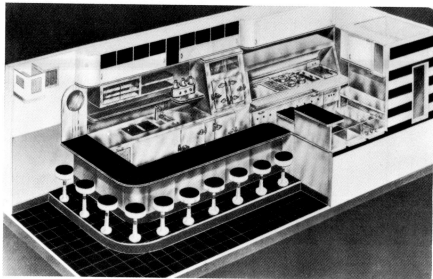

The Castle Turret and Davis' Diner were economy dinettes produced in the late 1930s by the Kullman Dining Car Company. Competing directly with the White Tower and White Castle hamburger trade, these small units occupied the middle ground between regular lunch room and large dining car.

In 1938 in Wichita, Kansas, the Valentine Manufacturing Company began to make prefab diners and sandwich shops. Unlike most manufacturers, they were not descended from the horsedrawn lunch wagon tradition, and their designs were generally a fresh departure. The standard Valentine had a skin of porcelain enamel in two colors. It was a boxy little building that sometimes incorporated scaled-down flying buttresses at the corners. Their nonspecialized shape made them very appealing, and Valentine built some liquor stores, shoe repair shops and bakeries that looked just like the diners.

Dinettes made a second comeback in the late 1940s, when many a returning vet aspired to the dining car business but couldn't swing the initial investment in the new jumbo diners. The Kullman Company introduced the Kullman Junior, stating in its sales brochure, "It brings you all the tested features of a super diner . . . boiled down to every-day needs." Whereas the Junior had all the equipment of the larger Kullman diners, enabling the customer to select from a full menu, other dinettes such as the White Star and the Paramount Short Stop were geared for short order trade only.

Mobile dinettes started to pop up more frequently after World War II, following the crowds to sports events and Sunday School picnics. Some of these miniature restaurants-on-wheels were set up permanently near shopping districts and railroad stations, while others moved around from plant to plant to feed the factory workers, a *modus operandi* highly reminiscent of the first quick lunch wagons.

THE BIRTH OF MODERNISM

1919 - 1932

The 1920s was an age of excitement and striking social change. It was also an age of materialism. Advertising came into its own, as literally thousands of new and redesigned products were offered to the hungry public—everything from new cars in gleaming new colors to shining new kitchens tiled in pristine white. Furniture and fashion went hand in hand, subject to changing whims of both the designers and the buyers.

The United States was riding high on the building boom that followed the Great War. With the proliferation of the automobile, Americans thronged to the suburbs, where a new way of life was beginning to take hold. The very lifestyle, free and easy, saw a throwing off of Victorian heaviness. Just as the rigid dress of the Victorian era was simplified and loosened, so too was the architecture. In the words of Walter Dorwin Teague, a leading designer of the modern era soon to come, "Our architecture became as clean-shaven as our chins."

It was a time of great change, extreme experimentation and diverse styles. Gradually, people began to realize that they didn't care to put up with what had been comfortable for their parents or grandparents. They came to dislike walls encrusted with elaborate plaster-work and carved wood ornaments that would better serve on wedding cakes. People wanted to live in surroundings that reflected the changing social scene. Modernism called for a total break with the past—no looking backward for design precedents. Designers tried to create contemporary styles to go with the new pace of living. To do so, they drew upon the example of machinery, where the design was purely functional—automobiles, airplanes and ocean liners . . . even grain elevators. This extreme functionalism was readily applied to architecture.

Modernism started in the twenties, but did not take deep hold until the Depression. Department stores, trying, as usual, to capture attention, were among the first to introduce the new designs in the late 1920s. But though a few fashionable and fashion-setting clients bought the new modern furniture, the majority of Americans were still fearful about experimenting within the sacred domain of their own homes. For quite a few years, most people continued to fill their houses with the same old mohair-covered, over-stuffed suites of furniture and the same fussy decoration. Modernism's most important early appearances, therefore, were in public spaces—hotel lobbies, railroad stations, offices and commercial buildings.

Fads and gimmicks were earmarks of the turbulent twenties. Novelties were devised continually to catch the public's fancy, especially on the crowded highways. Objects were blown up to ridiculous size in order to lure customers: massive coffee pots and enormous ice cream freezers, colossal tamales and king-sized brown derbies. This giant pig in Harlingen, Texas, offered pig or beef Bar-B-Q sandwiches. Diners, with their vehicular look, were also novelties—unusual places in which to grab a bite.

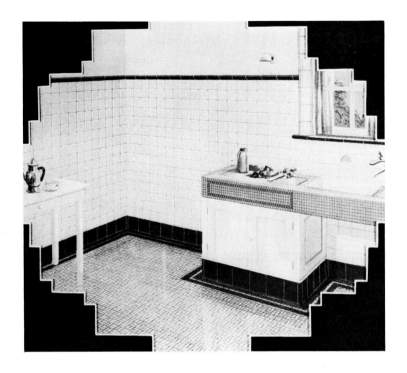

Kitchens in the home and kitchen areas in lunch cars took on a new, efficient all-tile look. Home kitchens became machines for food preparation—with a predominance of white to enhance the image of cleanliness. "Sno-White" tables and breakfast suites in stain-resistant enamel or "The White House Line" of gleaming kitchen and pantry units projected an air of modernity for which every homemaker hungered.

As diners grew bigger and bigger, they were forced to abandon the old wagon look. Continuing in a vehicle tradition, though, up-to-date inspiration was provided by the electric trolley or streetcar. As with real trolleys, the exterior trappings of the lunch wagons were greatly reduced. The relatively austere 1920s diner could even be compared to the Model T Ford, which has been described as a "naked, undisguised machine for transportation . . . free from extraneous ornament . . . perfectly suited to mass-production."

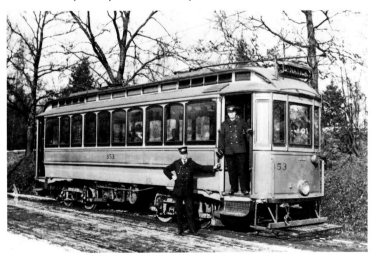

The transitional period following the First World War witnessed a mix of design from the Beaux-Arts tradition—something derived from historical precedent—to an urge to initiate new traditions, to be an era of origins and sources rather than a reworking of old imagery. These two pieces of furniture provide a good example of these conflicting styles. On the left is a grandfather's clock, manufactured by Philco, incorporating a radio. The cabinet is styled in Colonial Revival, with the clock face flanked by fluted pilasters and surmounted by a swan's neck pediment. The modern bookcase on the right was designed by Paul T. Frankl, one of the decade's leading decorators. His inspiration was the contemporary American city and its silhouette of skyscrapers—whose architectural design was completely up-to-date and totally American. Frankl described this piece as "rising up against the wall like some building against the sky."

The period's clean-cut modernism was not necessarily synonymous with a lack of adornment. The early twenties witnessed the first effects of the Art Deco style, itself influenced by cubism, ancient Egyptian, Aztec and American Indian art. Anything and everything could be found rendered in Art Deco—jewelry, furniture, clothing, entire buildings. Decorative floral fantasies covered walls, floors and furniture. Ornamental detailing on buildings followed suit. By the middle of the decade, these designs gave way to abstract geometrical ones, rectangular shapes with interlocking circles, polygons and ovals, zig-zags and oblique angles.

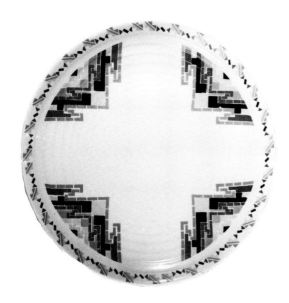

Streamliners

During the 1930s, as people discovered they were in the machine age, virtually every product on the market was redesigned with a new, futuristic, forward-looking styling. The streamlined look swept the nation, covering or housing thousands of everyday objects in smooth, teardrop-shaped packages.

The diner was no exception to the trend. The hard-edged box design of the twenties diners gave way to the newer look. Surfaces and textures were now brushed, polished, rounded or wrapped. In some cases the diners so thoroughly mimicked the sleek streamlined locomotives, which symbolized the era, that they actually brought about the immobilization of mobility. The more extreme applications of the new design ideas were not very widespread or long lived, but the concept of streamlining persisted for more than twenty-five years. All diners were affected by it, and over the next decade, especially, it came to be synonymous with modernization, as a more tempered version of streamlining dictated the character of diner design.

New graphics also played a part in creating a new image. The lettering of the Reading Diner in Reading, Massachusetts, typifies the decade of the 1930s. The Town Diner sign in Watertown, Massachusetts, used a scalloped design like water tumbling over rocks, also a thirties favorite.

Around 1940 a striking new diner style was produced by Sterling Diners of Merrimac, Massachusetts. Sterling's advertising expressed the design: "Just as the magic of streamlining has drawn thousands upon thousands of new customers to the streamliners of rail and air; just so the streamlined eye appeal of *Sterling Diners* never fails. . . . The sleek lines of Sterling Streamliners . . . practically shout, 'This MUST be a good place to eat.' " Streamlining was all a matter of imagery. The new style went way beyond questions of function or efficiency. It was applied purely as an aesthetic comment, important because it conveyed the of being up-to-date and forward-looking. This Sterling car, the Modern Diner, is in Pawtucket, Rhode Island.

The Worcester Lunch Car Company also built several streamliner diners. As with the Sterling Streamliners, this Worcester-made Mayflower diner in Quincy, Massachusetts, was designed with built-in forward motion. The feeling you got on entering a streamliner was unlike that of any ordinary diner: The flowing lines and airy quality invariably drew your eyes to one of the rounded ends.

The basic lines of the streamliners were never static, as arrows and other visual devices led the eye relentlessly forward. Even the sign, "Booth Service," leaned ahead as if in motion.

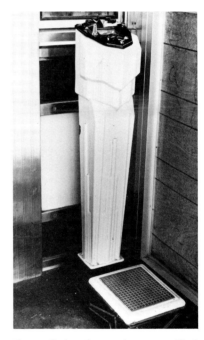

Worcester also built a large number of modified streamliners, such as the Pullman in Arlington, Massachusetts. The sloping sides of these toned-down models slanted inward up to the roof, and the corners were slightly rounded.

The vestibules of many diners were filled with vending machines echoing the new styling. This scale at Collins Diner in Canaan, Connecticut, is a highly angular example of the cascading water look.

41

New Materials for a New Era

The decade of the 1930s saw the emergence of many new materials, such as Formica, glass blocks, and stainless steel, which were immediately put to use in diner construction. Along with their contribution to the overall imagery, they helped to convey an idea of machine age efficiency and cleanliness. Materials in diners have always been selected for longevity and good appearance. Stainless steel, a tough, durable metal from which a variety of equipment could be made, achieved especially prominent use in the diner beginning in the mid-thirties. Soon entire backbars were made of it, becoming shining backdrops for attractive displays of food and food preparation.

Stainless was also used for a host of details and trim both inside and outside the diners. One example is this hood of Collins Diner in Canaan, Connecticut. Another is the housing for a light in Topps' Diner, Center Valley, Pennsylvania.

Glass blocks made their appearance around 1940, usually on the corners of diners. They provided an easy way to round off the corner and produced on the inside a nice, glowing light in the round corner booths.

The stainless steel backbar was a cinch to keep clean. A swipe with a damp cloth kept it gleaming, as Florence Barry demonstrated in 1940 at her father's Somerset Diner, Plainfield, New Jersey. The thin panels of steel were hand bent in presses, and the sunburst designs added strength and rigidity as well as a smart look.

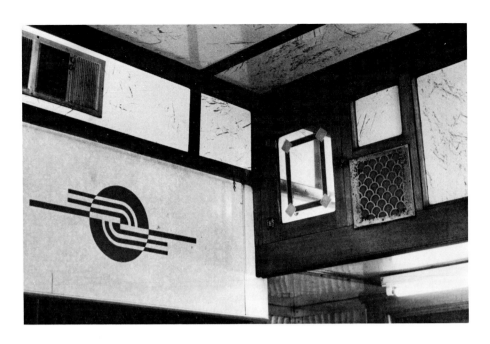

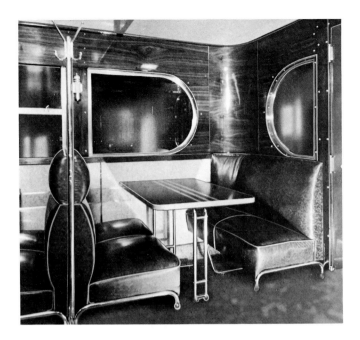

A new plastic material with the trade name Formica came into its own in the thirties and was used more and more frequently on the inside of diners as a burn-proof, acid-resistant material for counters and tabletops, replacing the traditional but much heavier and more costly marble. Formica wall and ceiling panels also helped to make the cleanup less tiresome. Inlaid Formica in colors brought individuality to many diners. The Silver Top Diner in Providence, Rhode Island, had silkscreened Formica panels as well as Formica in two colors inlaid into the mirrors. Art Deco or railroad motifs consisting of intersecting lines, circles and stripes were especially popular for tabletops. The interior shot of the booth, with the heavily padded seats and rounded, wood-paneled corner shows typical detailing and use of the new materials: Formica, chrome, stainless steel, leatherette and bent wood. Finally, on the exterior, one other material made its first diner appearance during the late thirties: neon. Soon brilliant signs were topping cars everywhere, along with multicolored piping running along many of the rooflines.

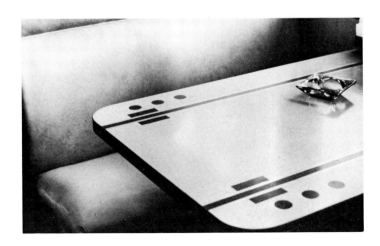

The Golden Age of the Diner

Talk with almost anyone about diners, and what pops into mind? Most people conjure up a railroad image—a long, low, sleek structure with an unbroken strip of windows, sheathed in glistening stainless steel or porcelain enamel. They're right. That is the look of the classic diners, those built just before and just after World War II. Their time was, without a doubt, the Golden Age of the Diner.

Because the war halted all production of new diners for several years, essentially the same models were built for nearly a decade. These were fluid-looking structures with no hard edges: all corners were rounded, including, in some cars, the corner windows. Ninety percent of the cars had table or booth service, as well as a counter. Fancy interior tilework had pretty much gone out the window, along with the use of such other expensive materials as marble, mahogany and leather. Such tilework as there was, was subdued. The new interiors were done in Formica, and the booths were framed in chrome tubing and covered with Naugahyde.

The demand for diners increased sharply after the war, as tens of thousands of veterans aspired to open up places of their own. These new civilians had plenty of cash—government loans or money they'd saved up during the war. But there was a shortage of some of the essential materials, such as Formica, steel and nickel, so at first the waiting period for new cars was up to a year or a year and a half.

By the late forties, however, things were back to normal, and there were more diners than ever. No fewer than twelve different companies were busy building them. Many of the older cars that had survived the lean war years were traded in on the flashy new models, and before long the Golden Age style of diner proliferated along the highways and in the cities.

The classic diner of the Golden Age—such as this O'Mahony car—was as snappy inside as out. The railroad image was continued with a monitor-shaped ceiling, now in two-tone Formica, but it was augmented by chrome stools and lights, and counters tiled in contrasting colors.

One of the trademarks of dining car design in the 1940s was the generous use of reflective surfaces. The stainless steel backbar became a veritable visual center, picking up the light bouncing and flashing through the diner.

During the Golden Age of the Diner careful attention was paid to the total look, as all parts were designed to mesh into a single image. Of course, the new style did not emerge all at once, and this superb example from the late thirties still shows the Art Deco influence. Especially handsome are the tile floor, which creates an optical illusion, and its unique stools with their octagonal tops and fluted chrome bases. Formica is an important material in this car. It is used liberally, covering the counter and tabletops, the ceiling panels, and the backbar hood above.

Design ingenuity and a high level of craftsmanship combined during the Golden Age to turn an ordinary element like the entrance to a diner into an appealing special effect. In the forties, the doorway surmounted by a clock was the visual focus of many diners, drawing the customer right inside. In its simplest form, the entrance was a naked door with a mere overhang. From there it evolved into an elaborate vestibule made up of a variety of materials. On the inside, the clock was a distinguishing feature, set in intricate patterns of stainless steel.

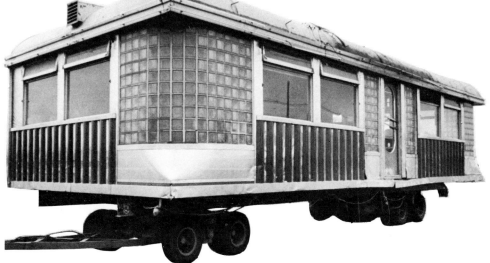

This unusual diner was built by Mountain View Diners, one of the new companies of the 1940s. It used all the standard materials of the day, porcelain enamel, stainless steel, and glass blocks, but it put them together in a unique way.

The late thirties Avenue Diner, built by the Jerry O'Mahony Company, was a clean, completely rounded porcelain enamel job, affecting the look of highly glazed earthenware. Diners like this one were built through the late 1940s.

Although the diner has always served as its own advertisement, the addition of the separate sign served not only to name or point out the place but also to individualize it. The owner could go beyond what he got from the factory and indulge his fancy. Here is a sampling.

This handsome car was manufactured by the Fodero Dining Car Company in 1946. Its sleek exterior sports thin alternating bands of stainless steel and two colors of porcelain enamel.

A diner built in 1940 by the Kullman Dining Car Company. Thin vertical panels of fluted porcelain make up the exterior, along with floor to ceiling glass blocks which rounded off the corners. The matching vestibule was also built at the factory.

There was one style of diner offered during the Golden Age that was different from all others. The Worcester Lunch Car Company kept producing its barrel-roofed car—the VW Beetle of diners—for more than thirty years. These models remained extremely popular in New England. The exterior employed flat porcelain enamel panels with the name of the diner baked in.

THE WORLD OF TOMORROW – TODAY

1933 - 1947

It was at the 1933 Chicago World's Fair, the Century of Progress Exposition, that the general public received its first exposure to modern design. At the model housing exhibit, "The Homes of Tomorrow," people saw in some of the designs a simplicity and a directness for which they were more than ready.

The modernist movement in America had been helped in part by the stock market crash of October 24, 1929. By the early thirties, "a third of a nation" was poorly housed and underfed. The building industry had ground to a halt. Skyscrapers stood half-finished. The countryside was dotted with "Hoovervilles"—makeshift communities where the poor lived in shacks made from packing crates and cardboard boxes, some of them covered with old license plates and wallpapered with magazine ads.

When government housing projects were initiated to provide adequate shelter for those who lived in the shanty towns, the designers turned to modernism for their inspiration. Things had to get better, and here was a new architecture, forward-looking and optimistic. Large numbers of these functional houses with their simple lines and flat roofs were turned out.

Inside America's new homes, the modern style provided a spare, almost stark, backdrop for simply designed furniture. Whereas the goal of machine-made furniture a few decades earlier had been to look handmade, now the more machine-like it was, the better. This new vision of beauty came from the perfection of surface and line that could be gotten only by machine manufacture.

In the 1930s, the ultimate machine was, of course, the airplane. The very symbol of speed, it helped launch the whole era of streamlining—the new design concept that imprinted mobility on every object imaginable, movable or not. In the thirties and early forties, angular shapes of the twenties were softened with gentle, flowing curves. In the case of the airplane, the design was one intended to make for the least amount of air resistance. Similarly, locomotives and automobiles were encased in smooth skins in order that they might achieve greater speed more efficiently. Before long, however, vacuum cleaners, irons and other everyday objects were beginning to be streamlined as a part of the new look. This marked the end of purely functional design. When applied to household appliances and other items that weren't going anywhere, streamlining was obviously pure packaging.

This Coca-Cola bottling plant in Los Angeles was designed by Robert W. Derran in 1937. It is a classic example of thirties borrowed imagery, combining the popular streamline design with portholes, ship's railings, and other allusions to nautical architecture.

A number of experimental automobiles based on streamlining principles appeared during the 1930s. The Scarab, produced in 1935 by William Stout, was one of the most advanced vehicles one could purchase. The inside floor area was seven and a half feet long by five feet seven inches wide. The rear seat was convertible to a full-length couch. A table for cards or dining was included. Scarab's advertisements prophesied that it would "set all future styles in motorcars." Demonstrations were given upon invitation only.

Thirties homes were filled with streamlined objects of every description. An airplane table lamp with a fuselage of blue glass glowed when lit. A brooch, designed in the airline aesthetic, took the form of an engine and propeller. Streamlined salt and pepper shakers operated efficiently on the dinner table, and the refrigerator held sleek pitchers, butter dishes and other containers. One could also have a winged iron that nearly propelled itself, as well as a toaster so streamlined it looked as if it had arrived from outer space.

The influence of locomotive design in the 1930s was widespread. In the case of the Sterling Streamliner in Philadelphia (above), the owner carried the imagery to an outrageous extreme. He built his kitchen in the form of a railway tunnel from which the diner was meant to be racing. The Streamline Railway (below) was a child's pull toy—the same design on a different scale.

Not all modern design was streamlined. Jim's Restaurant, for example, was contemporary, but very angular. It is marked by the use of a very flashy new material: the opaque colored glass known as Vitrolite, in contrasting colors. This Sunoco station (right) used the same materials but went the opposite route. A sweeping curved corner design created a radically streamlined facade.

This 1936 Pullman observation car shows interior streamlining at its best. The Pullman people had the good sense to leave the possibly out-of-place but extremely comfortable overstuffed chairs. Everything else, though, is perfect. The ash trays couldn't be rounder nor the end of the car more bullet shaped. Inlaid Formica, lots of shining chrome, and luxuriously curved surfaces all contribute to the car's sleek design.

A Place to Take the Kids

In the 1950s, diners began to move from their downtown sites to the suburban communities, where people had more money and tended to eat out more often. By this time, diners had grown tremendously in popularity and respectability, and the owners of these new cars were making a special effort to get the family trade. They were grand places, most of them, fancy enough to make dining out a real treat but still light enough on the pocketbook to let it become a regular habit. In some of the cars, the kids enjoyed their own special menus, as well as free balloons and lollipops dispensed on the way out. A great many of the parents brought their children back—or maybe it was the other way around.

Of course diners had to grow a little to handle the family crowds, and as a result many of them lost their special cozy atmosphere. Some were now seating as many as 150 or 200 people, which required huge separate dining areas. But even if you sat at the counter, things were no longer quite the same. The short order cook had moved behind closed doors to a big kitchen annex in the back and the customer was no longer where the action was. Counter showmanship, good, inexpensive entertainment, was a thing of the past, now to be found only in older cars.

The outside look of the diner was also subtly, but unmistakably, changing. Most visibly the railroad-style monitor roof, a diner element for twenty-five years, was on the way out. It wasn't needed any more to provide light and ventilation, and not only that, it just didn't fit in with the new image. The railroad look was no longer considered up-to-date, and dinermen wanted their places to appear and feel more like regular restaurants. The new trend was the "wide open" look, as the windows were enlarged to picture-window size. When the diners were lit up at night, they became their own advertisements as warm, cheery havens, and passersby were drawn right on in.

Ponzio's Brooklawn Diner in Brooklawn, New Jersey, was built by Kullman in the late forties and shows the old diner styling undergoing distinct growing pains. Although it doesn't look it from the outside, this diner could seat 105 customers. But that was just about the maximum capacity that could be packaged in this old form. The billowing monitor roof, seen below from the inside, had clearly outlived its usefulness, so a row of saucer-like air conditioning ducts alternated with glowing light fixtures down the center. The name of Ponzio has been associated with well-known popular diners for fifty years; the Brooklawn was the last one that patriarch James J. Ponzio operated before his death.

The early fifties diners were beginning to break away to something new, but to the untrained eye most still appeared relatively unchanged. In the 1952 Fodero-built Pisano's 74th St. Diner, the monitor roof was gone, but the base of the sign became its visual replacement, almost as if it wanted to hang on to the railroad styling. Pisano's sat up a couple of feet on a fairly flashy fieldstone foundation with those semi-circular red brick steps almost reaching right out at you.

The spirit of rejoicing in the advances of technology was irrepressible. The diners of the fifties were unified creations with elegant bands of steel and glass, generous use of sweeping curves and hidden sources of glowing light.

The eating public usually preferred to patronize newer diners, so older ones like the Franklin were traded in. In this unusual old-and-new picture, it can be clearly seen how the new diner renounced the outdated monitor roof. The railroad car look disappeared, and the imagery shifted to that of a well-tooled machine.

Dolly's Diner featured something that few of the older diners had, but most newer models were sure to include: a factory-built kitchen hooked right on the back. By 1950 no one ever had to construct a cinderblock kitchen annex for his car. The matching kitchen was convenient and gave the diner a new unified look.

55

By the mid-fifties diner-restaurants were where the real action was, in huge set-ups like the Country Club on Rt. 309 north of Philadelphia. Diners of this size could easily accommodate 125 patrons and were built in four or five sections. The dining area itself was 24 feet wide and 34 feet long. Menus in places such as these had become as long as your arm, some running six pages or more. You could now get such fare as lobster Cantonese, crêpes suzette and champagne, although a customer was still in, fed and out again in an average time of twenty minutes.

Like the automobiles of the era, the deluxe diners gave rise to all sorts of new gadgets and accessories. Some diner customers might well have been confronted with a Robot Cashier. Merely a coin-receiving device, this gimmick eliminated the human element in bill paying. The addition of a "Nab Diner" cookie and cracker dispenser to any diner would enable patrons to nibble a Nab for a nickel—and the owner to pick up a few extra cents. On the way out, they might also have stopped to pluck a toothpick from the Gits toothpick dispenser—bullet shaped, sanitary, and designed with definite eye appeal.

Who could ever pass by without stopping at Swingles' Diner on Route 22 in Springfield, New Jersey? The big picture windows fairly beckoned you inside the brightly lit premises. Outdoor lights and a big, flashy neon sign pulled you right off the highway into the spacious asphalt parking lot.

Patrons of the Nite Owl Diner in Fall River, Massachusetts, had their choice of two different diner atmospheres after the arrival in 1956 of a new companion Nite Owl Diner. Anyone could see things had come a long way from those early days of the tiny crowded lunch wagon. Needless to say, even as a curiosity piece, the old wagon couldn't compete in popularity, and it was soon removed.

This view (right) of the Plain and Fancy Diner in Allentown, Pennsylvania, shows clearly why it wasn't much fun to sit at the counter anymore. All you could see was pie displays, brewing coffee and maybe a milkshake mixing away. All the real cooking took place behind those closed doors with the portholes. On the other hand, the homey touches were stronger than ever—curtains, chandeliers, wood grain and tile.

The Diner Blasts Off

The incredible futuristic diners of the early sixties were clearly the offspring of the space age. Great juggernauts of stainless steel, tile and glass, they had an undeniably new look. Their identifying feature was their roofline—a bizarre zig-zag canopy that looked as if it had been cut out with a gigantic pair of pinking shears. The diners didn't really bear much resemblance to manned rocket ships or lunar modules, but they did reflect—with exuberance—the new technologies of the sixties. The vigor of the space age as seen in diners was akin to the public's keen interest in the push to the moon. As always, new materials were showcased in the diners, and builders rarely failed to point out that they were innovators in the same tradition as the aerospace industry. Not precisely the stuff of rocket flights, the new diner materials of this period included beach pebble marble imported from Italy, bamboo draw curtains, and handsome light fixtures that looked like little flying saucers. Still, these diners were progressive and had a far-out look all their own.

The Peter Pan Diner in Brightwaters, Long Island, built in the late fifties, marked the transition into the space age. In this case the new look was confined to the vestibule, which was capped with a flared canopy reaching upward and outward.

The Bordentown Grill & Bar in Bordentown, New Jersey, saw the spread of the folded plate roofline around the entire diner. Even on the inside, through the windows, you can see a zig-zagging hood over the backbar. The diner floated above the cars in the parking lot on a flagstone and tile base.

The Skyliner Diner was another late sixties variation on the space theme, mostly glass with an enormous vestibule/waiting room pierced by a giant, skyward-pointing triangle framing the doors. The snaking canopy was dotted with spotlights like so many stars in the heavens.

This advertisement by Manno Dining Car Company clearly emphasized the space age connection as the planets float around the diner, itself situated in the vortex of the Milky Way.

The Starlite on Route 1 in Penndel, Pennsylvania, could perhaps be called the ultimate space age diner, with maybe a little medieval cathedral thrown in. It was not a factory-built job; the owner rehabbed an older diner himself, trying to keep up with the tastes of the times.

POSTWAR RAZZLE-DAZZLE

1948-1962

The Second World War left the United States with a severe housing shortage. To deal with this problem, entrepreneurial builders began turning out housing developments on an unheard-of scale—whole communities were mass-produced with look-alike houses that might even include look-alike shrubbery out front. By 1951, Levittown, New York, begun six years earlier on a potato farm, had 17,447 carbon-copy houses. South of San Francisco, Daly City consisted in the 1950s of thousands of $6,000 boxy houses built five feet apart.

This was the decade in which the ranch house became *the* suburban dwelling unit. All ranches were basically the same—one level, with a flat or slightly sloping roof, and a big picture window. Although similar on the outside, these houses were personalized on the inside by their owners. Two decors were prevalent: Early American and contemporary. The former included reproduction antiques along with a brick fireplace, accented by a huge copper frying pan hanging as an ornament. Gigantic modern spoon and fork sets were also *de rigueur.* Braided rugs added a feeling of hominess and just the right amount of informality. The contemporary, on the other hand, had low, comfortable furniture, frequently with wrought iron legs. Favorite shapes caught the contemporary public's fancy—the boomerang and amoeba could be found imposed upon coffee tables, in rug designs, on wallpaper and on Formica countertops. And don't forget the kidney-shaped pool out back.

The exploration of outer space was responsible for yet another widespread look in everyday design, as a multitude of buildings and products appeared with skyward-pointing angled surfaces. The space race could be seen in automobile design as a tail fin race—who could produce the most outlandish rocket-like rear end?

Color coordination was a focus of the well-designed interior. Tints and shades of one's favorite color were used to extremes. Pink, pinky-beige, muted brick-red and rosy red could all be found in the same living room. Other favorites were turquoise, coral, tangerine and charcoal. Black and white in checkerboard or stripes were also popular, with splashes of yellow or orange thrown in.

The TV room, also known as the rec room, grew more popular every year. Dedicated to family leisure, it might sometimes feature a shuffleboard court inlaid in its linoleum floor. The bar and the game table were ubiquitous.

The new postwar suburbs reflected a growing homogeneity across the United States. In the fifties, Sears, Roebuck stopped printing its special catalogs for the different regions of the country. People everywhere were beginning to like much the same things. Better communications—more glossy magazines and a lot of television—undoubtedly paved the way. Products formerly advertised locally were now pushed nationwide. It was the beginning of yet another period of unprecedented well-being.

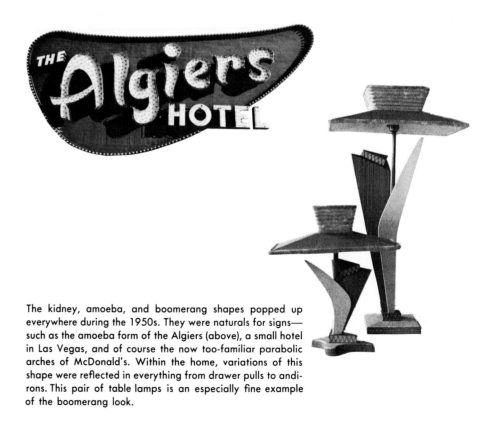

The kidney, amoeba, and boomerang shapes popped up everywhere during the 1950s. They were naturals for signs—such as the amoeba form of the Algiers (above), a small hotel in Las Vegas, and of course the now too-familiar parabolic arches of McDonald's. Within the home, variations of this shape were reflected in everything from drawer pulls to andirons. This pair of table lamps is an especially fine example of the boomerang look.

The 1959 Chevrolet sported a classic rear end: flared, sweeping tail fins, buttoned down over the license plate.

The Stardust Casino in Las Vegas went whole hog on a space theme. The entire facade is a giant starburst, complete with floating planets and glittering stars amid the pointy letters.

This children's library addition to the public library in Natick, Massachusetts, reveals a more down-to-earth version of the jagged look of the late fifties and early sixties. The folded plate roof became very popular, as did the flared canopy with recessed lights over the glass-enclosed vestibule.

Mister Donut used a sign in the shape of its folded plate zig-zag roof.

Neba and Mike's are a couple of fast food joints from the early sixties in Albany, New York. Their look appears to be a McDonald's derivative—lots of back-lit Plexiglas, great expanses of glass and a foundation of mosaic tile, not to mention the arches.

The Lido Diner in Springfield, New Jersey, built in 1960, shows marked 1950s influences. The space age look is reflected in the many canted surfaces, the flared canopy and the vestibule roofline. Glass and multi-colored mosaic tile are dominant materials.

Not a Diner But a Restaurant

In 1962 the Kullman Dining Car Company of Newark, New Jersey, built the first Colonial-style diner in Ocean City, New Jersey. It had an exterior of brick, punctuated with bay windows and coach lamps, and the inside featured a plethora of plastic-laminate wood-grain panelings. The era of the stainless steel diner was coming to a close. From this time, nearly all diners were built of brick and stone.

With the widespread urban renewal projects that ushered in the 1960s came scores of city planning boards, who began to legislate taste in buildings. This was an ominous sign for diners, as the old flashy look was no longer tolerated. All new diners had to conform to stringent regulations, which often banned not only stainless steel buildings, but even the word "diner." As Harold Kullman so confusingly put it in an interview, "We designed a brick *diner* that wasn't a *diner,* but a restaurant. . . ." Not a diner, but a restaurant . . .

In fact, all these new Colonial diners are still diners, no matter what the sign out front says, and no matter how they look on the outside. A diner has always been and continues to be a pre-fabricated restaurant with counter service, built in sections in a factory and transported to a distant site. Even though a typical new diner may consist of thirteen sections, containing a vestibule, a coat room, a bake shop, a display area, a cocktail lounge, two dining rooms and a kitchen, it will still have a "diner area," complete with a counter and stools facing a battery of gleaming fountain equipment, pie cases and coffee urns. That is how it began, and that is how it still is.

Yet, as Michael Loizos, one of the owners of the L & M Diner-Restaurant in Ocean Township, New Jersey, observed one day, as he stood pushing the button on his diner's automated, electric-driven coat rack, "Today the diner is not the pie wagon it used to be."

These are typical of the earliest Colonial diner designs, dating from 1962. The outside conformed to the boxy look of the period, except for the brick and the bay windows. Inside, wagon wheels and wood grain Formica provided a rustication that was well suited to the Early American motif.

By the mid-sixties the rage for Colonial diners spawned a host of historical revival styles. It was a time of "anything goes." The manufacturers combined a myriad of building motifs, and the details were usually mixed together with freestyle whimsy: Greek columns with Egyptian mosaic wall murals and an Early American ornamental balustrade topping off the roof. The 1967 Empress Diner (above left) in Fairlawn, New Jersey, was a kind of ultimate in classical design, with its facade of Ionic half-columns applied over the window supports, not really resting on the foundation, just more or less hanging there in mid-air. Ed's (center left) in Newark, New Jersey, on the other hand, showed no such consistency of style, though a Tudor look, with its half-timbered wall panels, was predominant. Marty's Place (below left) has a coherent architectural look to it, even if it's only a box with a little box out front as the entrance. However, the Colonial (above) remained the odds-on favorite for ten years, and many an interior was jazzed up with wagon wheel lights and saddle-as-wall-hanging. Others employed rifles over the fireplaces, gunbelts, Indian statues, cowboy boots, and brown and white spotted Naugahyde cowhide.

Diner dining rooms ranged from somewhat cozy rec room styled spaces with fireplaces and wood paneling all the way to giant ballroom-sized expanses with crystal chandeliers, paintings, sculptured busts and bas-reliefs.

The L & M Diner in Ocean Township, New Jersey (circa 1967), made by Kullman, is an example of the most recent, and now most popular, historical revival style: the Mediterranean. The exterior consists of repetitive arched bays supported by slanted fins, all of white stucco. At night the diner is dramatically lit—each bay has its own spotlight.

They really went crazy with the classical theme on the inside of the L & M Diner. The back wall was the focus of the dining room, with a colonnade filled with statuary of the muses. A few Roman busts were also scattered around the diner. The crystal chandeliers gave the right look, but did little of the real lighting; the usable light came from spots recessed in the ceiling.

Zoto's in Line Lexington, Pennsylvania, is the Fodero Dining Car Company's mid-seventies Mediterranean entry. The windows are nicely edged in brick, and protruding beams (mission style) appear to hold up their Spanish quarry tile mansard roof.

This mid-1970s interior done by the De Raffele Manufacturing Company shows the latest styling and looks like an attempt to use every material that nature and science can provide. The dining room is chock full of tufted Naugahyde, imitation Tiffany lamps, ornate wall plaques, hurricane and coach lamp chandeliers, and indoor/outdoor carpeting. The slightly manic look is that of an overdone family play room styled by a too-zealous interior decorator.

The Rage for Renovation

What happens to a diner that is going out of style? Back in the old days, it would be traded in on a newer model, but today's diners have grown so big and so costly that, more often than not, a trade-in is unfeasible.

Occasionally an older diner is recognized as something special, something that's not really going out of style, but which should be kept up and preserved. But, sadly, more common is the view that what's needed is renovation, and many vintage diners today are being "redone." This "redoing" runs the gamut from merely adding a new roof to a complete coverup of the old diner with new materials.

The reasoning behind renovation is simply to make the car look less like a diner to passersby. Frequently the interior remains unchanged while a whole new image is slipped over the outside. Owners often operate under the impression that the public no longer cares for old diners, when the opposite may more often be the case. Time and again, local townspeople feel a sense of real loss when their favorite old place is adulterated in the name of progress.

The owner of the Village Diner in Grand Gorge, New York, was plagued by a leaky ceiling. His answer to the problem was to tack on a traditional pitched roof, covering up the old railroad-style monitor roof. Oddly, he left the rest of his 1942 porcelain enamel diner intact.

Even the newer diners have not been immune to the passion for renovation. This late sixties Colonial diner in West Orange, New Jersey, was transformed into Fong's Garden by the addition of several layers of custom-built pagoda-like rooflines.

The original beauty of this 1940 diner in Providence, Rhode Island, is evidenced only in the edging of orange stained glass that trims the windows. The rest of it is completely obliterated by a row of paste-on columns and turquoise panels that box in the entranceway and ends.

BEFORE

BEFORE

The Maple in Elizabeth, New Jersey, was once (above) a classic 1940s all-stainless steel diner with rounded glass block corners. Now (below) the entrance has been sheared off and moved to the side so the street facade can be a continuous row of brick arches set in stone and framing the windows. The gleaming stainless machine has become a mansarded Mediterranean villa.

Lindholm's Diner (above), a stunning 1941 Streamliner, was once a well-known landmark in Rutland, Vermont, but few today would recognize it from the outside. Encased in brick and wood, it has been reborn as Minard's Family Restaurant (below). Incredibly, its unique streamliner interior remains intact, a poignant reminder of what it used to be.

AFTER

AFTER

Echoes of the Past

The need for meals on wheels has by no means disappeared. Following in the tradition of the very first lunch wagons, many modern-day mobile eateries continue to feed the public. Some are true diner creations, built in dining car factories and specially fitted to pickup truck bodies. These are direct descendants from horsedrawn night lunch cars, pulling into the center of town at dusk and setting up in the very same spots as their forebears. Other mealmobiles are simply stainless steel food-dispensing units slapped onto the backs of pickups. Daily, thousands of these make the rounds of businesses and factories peddling sandwiches, coffee and donuts. The quick lunch business has, it seems, come full circle. The diners have outgrown, for the most part, the capability to go to where the business is, so a whole new crop of mobile lunches has appeared to fill the need.

The Haven Brothers mobile diner, built inside a converted tractor trailer, is a nightly fixture in Providence, Rhode Island. Excepting only local hotels, it can safely claim to be the oldest restaurant in town. The first Haven Brothers diner opened for business in a T. H. Buckley-built White House Café in 1893.

A familiar and welcome sight to millions of workers every day is the coffee truck. Arriving on a regular schedule and staying but a few minutes, the truck's simple fare cheers and satisfies.

Jack Hickey plies his trade from a truck-mounted Worcester Lunch Car at the Common in Taunton, Massachusetts. His 1947 model replaced one that was still drawn by horse up to that year. It is the only wagon left of four that once parked at each corner of the square.

This little van makes its appearance only for special events, such as this sidewalk sale in Emmaus, Pennsylvania. But you can be sure you'll find one at any state or county fair and maybe even at a championship Little League game.

Ollie's Trolley is really the next step after mobile lunches. Just like the first permanently moored but still portable lunch wagons, Ollie's, in Fairfax, Virginia, is a self-contained prefab restaurant, even adopting the imagery of the old trolley-style lunch cars.

Mike's Diner also pulls into Providence every evening. It is shown here on the road, moving from its daytime parking spot into the city. (The truck is barely visible behind the bushes.) This version of Mike's was built in 1965 after the previous one just plain wore out.

GILLEY'S

Ralph "Gilley" Gilbert ran the operation of this eleven-stool lunch cart in Portsmouth, New Hampshire, for forty years, and every night for those forty years it was parked illegally in Market Square. In time, Gilley accumulated more than 5000 parking tickets, thereby earning himself a place in the *Guinness Book of Records*. According to legend, the fifty-cent nightly fine was usually balanced off by the issuing officer's settling in for coffee and a piece of pie.

When Gilley finally retired in 1974, the town, knowing it was the end of an era, honored him with a parade. A local ordinance assured that no one would be allowed to take over his diner and bring it nightly into the middle of town.

Gilley's Lunch Cart is now moored permanently in a nearby parking lot. Steve Geno, a part-time taxi driver using an adjacent spot to wait for fares, noticed that people were continually going up to the diner, not knowing it was closed. Soon he arranged to open it again as an immobile lunch wagon, keeping its old late night hours and its famous name. It is owned by John Murray, and he and Steve do a thriving business. Gilley himself, unable to stay away, comes down to lend a hand from time to time.

LOOKING BACKWARD...AGAIN

1963 -

Since the early 1960s, popular design has immersed itself in a myriad of historical revival styles. The most favored has certainly been Colonial, or Early American; others include Mediterranean, Tudor and French Mansardic. More often than not, these styles have been mixed and mismatched in one astonishing conglomeration after the next.

After forty years or so of futuristic design, the current trend to revivalism represents a significant departure. Contemporary design continues, of course, but more often than not, popular design in the last two decades has brought back and reworked favorite motifs from the past.

The rusticated Colonial look appears in innumerable thousands of homes and businesses, with its variably authentic offerings of coach lamps, thick pine furniture, wagon wheel fixtures and plastic-laminate wood-grain paneling. Each of the other styles has its identifying features: Mediterranean—a row of repeating archways and the use of stucco; Tudor—half-timbering, what else?; Mansardic—a new version of the seventeenth-century mansard roof, usually with a flat top and steeply sloping sides which are a continuation of the roof onto the facade.

Why the current revival should have come about when it did is not clear. Perhaps it is that the sixties and seventies were a period of such sharp change and such bitter disillusionment that people felt more secure reaching back to remembered styles. In any event, the ever-growing desire to hold onto the past, while living in the present, has also created a new awareness of existing resources. Happily, restoration and adaptive reuse of older structures has sometimes become more attractive than tearing down and building anew. This has even been the case with diners. A few older-vintage cars have been given new life by concerned citizens who would rather not see them bulldozed and disappear. One classic place, the Modern Diner in Pawtucket, Rhode Island (see page 40), has recently been placed in the National Register of Historic Places.

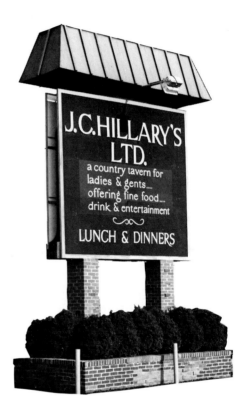

Mansard mania hit America in the sixties and continues un-checked today. It started innocently enough as an honest revival, but soon went on the rampage, resulting in mansardic hats for McDonald's, gas stations, supermarkets, apartment complexes, and even light fixtures. There's got to be a man-sarded mailbox out there somewhere.

For some reason, the Tudor revival of the past two decades has generally been accomplished with much greater taste than the mansarding of America. For one thing, it is usually much more integrated into the total design of the building. The Sheraton Tara Hotel (left) in Framingham, Massachusetts, even has a Tudor bus stop (right) to go along with it. In the case of a house in Medfield, Massachusetts (lower left), the design is a bit more muddied, with the addition of familiar Colonial features. Predictably, the mansard has been combined with the Tudor, and a dreary example is this florist shop (lower right) in Dedham, Massachusetts.

The past decade has seen a proliferation of log cabin homes. This spacious Massachusetts home in rugged pioneer style couldn't be further removed from its predecessor in size and design. Among its features are two stories of living space, a full basement, and an attached two-car log garage (partially hidden by the frontier-spirited four-wheel-drive vehicle).

This Mediterranean bus stop is easily identified by its quarry tile roof and arched porticos in stucco. Though it might seem out of place in Malden, Massachusetts, it serves a large condominium complex, the Granada, which also affects a Spanish style.

Who knows if anyone in the Old West ever actually perched a passel of lanterns on a wagon wheel and used it as a chandelier? But that's not the point. Today the wheel has become a favorite rustic light fixture, bringing that frontier spirit right home.

The nationwide Friendly's ice cream chain stores are done in a tasteful Colonial style. Here the carry out window is flanked by slightly shrunken vestigial shutters that double as ice cream flavor menu boards.

Texaco has taken to domesticating its gas stations, turning them into coy variations on a Cape Cod style. The sign is highlighted within a foreshortened gable and the roof is punctuated by three fake dormer windows over the belanterned service bays.

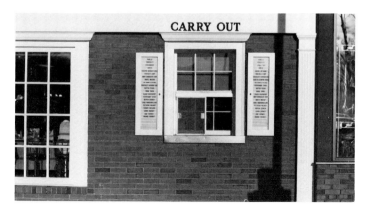

Diners
and
Diner People

THREE PHOTOGRAPHIC PORTFOLIOS

BY ELLIOTT KAUFMAN

I

II

III

Picture Credits